SUICIDE

A CRY FOR HELP

Helen Hosier

SUICIDE

A CRY FOR HELP

Helen Hosier

Harvest House Publishers
Irvine, California 92714

Scripture quotations marked NASB are from the NEW AMERICAN STANDARD BIBLE, copyright © The Lockman Foundation 1960, 1962, 1963, 1968, 1971, 1972, 1973, 1975 and are used by permission.

Scripture quotations marked KJV are from the KING JAMES VERSION.

All other Scripture quotations are from THE LIVING BIBLE, copyright © 1971, Tyndale House Publishers, Wheaton, Illinois. Used by permission.

SUICIDE, A CRY FOR HELP

Table of Contents

Preface

Suicide! The whispered word. The taboo subject. "Going sideways," young people call it today. By any name it is ugly and unnecessary—an insult to humanity, the community, and society.

Suicide is a problem growing in intensity, and no one is immune. Suicide appears in all ages, in both sexes, and on every economic level, with no geographic boundaries.

The seriousness of the suicide problem has hit me as I have read letters relating suicide attempts or accounts of completed suicides and as I have faced the magnitude of the problem of depression and its devastating consequences in my own life.

This book has been written—not because I particularly enjoyed examining this despressing and touchy subject but out of a sense of need, a sense of addressing myself to what I see as a growing problem.

This book offers understanding and sympathy to those so overwhelmed by the vicissitudes of life that they have sought escape through suicide but have failed in their attempt. It also examines motives and lays bare some facts that are often overlooked. I do this in a spirit of love and genuine concern.

Loving acceptance and open communication can move a person out of suicidal preoccupation when he is shown that there is hope and a reason for living. This I have tried to do. The psalmist asked, "O my soul, why be so gloomy and discouraged? Trust in God! Praise Him for His wondrous help; he will make [you] smile again" (Psalm 43:5). Yes, I *strongly* recommend this: "Hope in God" (Psalm 42:5).

1

An Eclipse in My Soul

I was tired beyond the telling, both physically and mentally. Every fiber of my being ached; nerves were taut; pressure had mounted to the exploding point; and depression had settled in like a heavy blanketing fog. My vision was obscured by the black pessimism of despair, and the future stretched before me as one long bout with loneliness. All I could see was work, loneliness, more work, and more lonely difficult hours of struggle. Work, loneliness, tiredness—the thoughts cycled through my mind in ceaseless repetition. Friends tried to be understanding, but no one really understood.

In the back of my mind hovered the knowledge that God understood. He cared; He comprehended. But I was so weary of it all. I had no doubt about the reality of God, but at this point I needed someone with flesh and bones. All I wanted was a shoulder to lean on; someone else to help carry the load besides God. I felt starved for love.

I drove thirty-five miles from my home under a mammoth weight of despair. Arriving at my destination, I felt alone, rejected and unwanted. I was totally incapable of rational thought as I reached into the glove compartment of the car and took out the unopened bottle of sleeping pills. There was a can of cola beside me. My last thought was a prayer: "God, forgive me, but I'd rather be with You."

Twelve hours later I awoke in my own bed. Was it a bad dream? A nightmare? No, I was fully clothed and in my hand was the bottle of sleeping pills, an empty bottle!

I was now a statistic—a living statistic, to be sure. And I was not sure I was happy about it. "You are a walking miracle," the doctor later declared. "The pills should have done it; and if they hadn't, the thirty-five mile freeway drive back to your home certainly should have taken care of your desire to end it all. I don't understand how you drove that car back. If I never believed in angels before, I certainly do now. Your guardian angel worked overtime! I have a feeling Someone up there wants you around alive awhile longer."

I was alive and comparatively well on planet Earth. Now what was I going to do? Had I really wanted a permanent out? My mind struggled with the question. But not all the time for there was work to do. Work! I hated the word. But it stared me in the face. Stacks of it. Work is always good therapy, I told myself, and so I pitched in.

I received help from loving, concerned friends, including a very knowledgeable psychologist. I tried laughing, joking somewhat, trying to look at my situation more objectively. I was surprised to discover that I could still smile, laugh and joke. There had been an eclipse in my soul. Long, dark shadows had fallen across my path. Midnight hours. I had experienced it. But the sun still rose each morning, the birds still chirped, awakening me and the day's work was there to greet me. "Count your blessings," I reminded myself; "work is a blessing, not your bane."

Then alone I retreated into the Psalms in the Bible. The psalmist became my companion. Strange, you say. You shake your fist in the face of God and try to kill yourself, and then you read the Bible. Strange perhaps, but true. I discovered that David, who wrote many of the psalms, had his highs and lows. In the crucible of daily living, David soared to heights of joy, and plummeted to the depths of despair. In his pilgrimage from doubt to certainty, in his conquest of despair, he laid bare his heart. I sought refuge and found the help I needed to sustain me through the difficult hours. The gamut of human experiences are reflected in those psalms— anguish and guilt, gloom and apprehension, fear, pain, grief, sadness and weariness—all this and much more spoke to my aching heart. And oh, how I identified. In my copy of *The Living Bible*, the book of Psalms is underlined and circled; there are exclamation points and little notes, all a solemn reminder, even today, that God had seen me and taken me through this crisis in my soul.

Some of those underlined excerpts read like this:

"Death bound me with chains, and the floods of ungodliness mounted a massive attack against me. Trapped and helpless, I struggled against the ropes that drew me on to death.

"In my distress I screamed to the Lord for his help. And he heard me from heaven, my cry reached his ears . . . he sped swiftly to my aid . . . Suddenly the brilliance of his presence broke through the clouds . . . He reached down from heaven and took me and drew me out of my great trials. He rescued me from deep waters. He delivered me . . .

" . . . the Lord held me steady. He led me to a place of safety, for he delights in me."

I remember stopping in my reading when I read, *"He delights in me"* Was it really true? *Me?* I knew the Bible was a timeless book; its very timelessness made it applicable to every age of history. So it did include *me.* I read on.

"You have turned on my light! The Lord my God has made my darkness turn to light. Now in your strength I can scale any wall, attack any troop.

"What a God he is! How perfect in every way! All his promises prove true. He is a shield for everyone who hides behind him. For who is God except our Lord? Who but he is as a rock?"

Oh, how I needed a strong rock to lean against. There followed long periods of anguish when I would pour out my heart to the God the psalmist said cares for me in my distress—to the God "Who is merciful."

"Lord! Help!

"Lord, lead me as you promised me you would . . . Tell me clearly what to do, which way to turn."

God was at work directing my turning. It was difficult. One does not jump up from trying to go sideways and immediately walk a straight, steady line. I limped, struggled, stumbled. Sometimes I fell down. Then again I would cry out like David:

"No, Lord! Don't punish me in the heat of your anger.

Pity me, O Lord, for I am weak. Heal me, for my body is sick, and I am upset and disturbed. My mind is filled with apprehension and with gloom. Oh, restore me soon.

" . . . every night my pillow is wet with tears . . . I am depending on you, O Lord my God."

It was not a misplaced dependence. God could be depended upon to heal the hurting me.

"Mark this well: The Lord will listen to me and answer when I call to him. Stand before the Lord in awe, and do not sin against him. Lie quietly upon your bed in silent meditation. Put your trust in the Lord, and offer him pleasing sacrifices. Many say that God will never help us. Prove them wrong, O Lord, by letting the light of your face shine down upon us . . . I will lie down in peace and sleep, for though I am alone, O Lord, you will keep me safe."

From one who has been there, you can take it as truth: He is a God Who helps; He is a God Who can be trusted; and He is a God Who keeps us safe. When we are alone, as so many are, He is a Reality.

I made many discoveries in those days coming up out of the pit of despair. The psalmist's mood in the Bible so often fit mine. He reflected my own spirit. There was release from my own deep inner hurt as I, with the writer, laid my wounded spirit at the feet of God.

I had been saved from myself. I began slowly to see that I was my own worst enemy; that in giving way to self-pity, and surrendering to black moods of oppression, I was shutting myself up to the love and help I so desperately craved. I needed to take myself in hand *and then hand myself over to God.* In those days, I caught myself saying, "Dear God, You are really getting the short end of this deal. I'm such a miserable bargain." Believe me, I found out that God doesn't mind!

David, in the Psalms, told me that God was my shield that He would defend me. I discovered that God is a judge Who is perfectly fair. Over and over again the psalmist told me that God is good, *so good.*

David said to this God of goodness, "I cannot understand how you can bother with mere puny man, to pay any attention to him!" (Psalm 8:4). That same thought frequently crossed my mind.

Out of the fullness of his heart David exclaimed, "O Lord, I will praise you with all my heart, and tell everyone about the marvelous things you do. I will be glad, yes, filled with joy because of you . . . You have vindicated me, you have endorsed my work, declaring from your throne that it is good" (Psalm 9:1-2, 4).

And to think that I had thought I needed someone else to help me carry the load besides God! Shame engulfed me, remorse for my foolish act.

"All who are oppressed may come to Him. He is a refuge for them in their times of trouble. All those who know your mercy, Lord, will count on you for help. For you have never yet forsaken those who trust in you" (Psalm 9:9-10).

David told me, "Tell the world about his unforgettable deeds" (Psalm 9:11b). I was a writer. Was God trying to get a message across to me? *You mean, God, You aren't through with me? You mean, I can still write and that someone will still publish for me?*

In my ears I was still hearing someone tell me, "You'll never be published again . . ." Now those words were becoming just a dim echo.

When David said that he felt helpless, overwhelmed, and in deep distress and that his problems seemed to go from bad to worse (Psalm 25:16), I, as a woman, alone, making the adjustment to a new job in a strange community, could feel some of the guilt about my own suicide attempt slip away. Here was "a man after God's own heart" making that kind of confession.

"See my sorrows; feel my pain; forgive my sins . . . Save me from them! Deliver [me] from their power! Oh, let it never be said that I trusted you in vain! . . . Assign me Godliness and Integrity as my bodyguards, for I expect you to protect me and to ransom [me] from all [my] troubles" (Psalm 25:18, 20-22).

In my mind's eye, I could see David lifting his hands to heaven imploring God's help. And just as God didn't ignore his cry, I knew He would help me, too. David, to our knowledge, did not make an attempt on his own life, but he must have felt like it many times. When you are the object of a schizophrenic king's hatred (King Saul, whose throne David took); when you are rejected by your countrymen and your favorite son (who tried to usurp your kingdom); when you lose your best friend; when you are faced with marital problems (and David had *many* wives); when you are confronted with your own sins and the magnitude of your own willfulness; when you are charged with the responsibility of having to make grave decisions of far-reaching importance; and when you have to face the death of loved ones, you will experience moments of deep anguish. Out of all this, David wrote the Psalms.

As I read God's response to David, the words of the doctor kept ringing in my head: *"You are a walking miracle . . . Someone up there wants you around alive for awhile yet."* It's good to be alive!

2

Could Something
Be Missing?

"Within the last year three of my friends tried to commit suicide. Life was too much for them. They couldn't hack it. This world ate them up until their only thought of escape was death. Could something be missing?"

So began a letter to the *Hollywood Free Paper*—only one of hundreds relating the same tragic story of attempted suicide or completed suicide. Could something be missing? That's a good question—the right question. People have been killing themselves since the beginning of recorded history, and it is safe to say that in every instance something has been missing.

There are many motives for suicide. Suicide is a complex problem and is becoming more so in our increasingly complex society. *But suicide is not the answer* to the complexity of problems and the anxieties of day to day living.

WHERE ARE YOU GOING?

Longing for death or contemplating suicide is not actually the ultimate in the "geographic cure." That a person is only changing one's location from earth to someplace else is an undeniable reality confirmed more and more in the many books now available relating the death experiences of scores of people. Most of these books would have the reader believe that at the end of the tunnel marked death there is this bright light and pleasurable experiences. All will be well in that "life beyond."

Dr. Maurice Rawlings, a specialist in internal medicine and cardiovascular diseases at the Diagnostic Hospital in Chattanooga, Tennessee, has documented a series of interviews with people who had been resuscitated—brought back to life after being clinically dead. What he found supports belief in life after death and the existence of a hell as well as heaven. In his book, *Beyond Death's Door,* Dr. Rawlings states: More and more of my patients who are recovering from serious illnesses tell me there is a life after death. There is a heaven and a hell. I had always thought of death as painless extinction. I had bet my life on it. Now I have had to reconsider my own destiny, and what I have found isn't good. I have found it really may not be safe to die!'' [2]

The turnabout in this doctor's life occurred when a patient had a cardiac arrest and dropped dead right in the doctor's office. In the process of resuscitating, as he regained his heartbeat and respiration, the man started screaming, ''I'm in hell.'' He was terrified and pleaded with the doctor to help him.

Dr. Rawlings worked feverishly and rapidly and the man's life was saved. In the process, however, both the patient and the doctor came to grips with the reality of hell. ''I had always dealt with death as a routine occurrence in my medical practice, regarding it as an extinction with no need for remorse or apprehension. Now I was convinced there was something about this life and death business after all. All of my concepts needed revision. I needed to find out more. It was like finding another piece in the puzzle that supports the truth of the Scriptures. I was discovering that the Bible was not merely a history book. Every word was turning out to be true.'' [3]

In the process of writing this book, it was my experience to meet and be in communication with a woman and her husband living in Minnesota. This couple had been struck by lightning and survived the horror of that experience, even though a direct hit is almost always fatal. An average volt of lightning can discharge as much as 100 million volts of energy and pack a wallop of one billion kilowatts of power. That this couple should survive was miraculous. Both of them relate the death tunnel experience, the bright Light and an encounter with the glory of God. But they also tell of falling away from this brilliant Light and knew they were not going to heaven. Something was missing in their lives, too.

One minister warned a would-be suicide, who was denying the reality of God and an eternity that would be spent in one of two places, that if he persisted in trying to take his own life, the place he would go to was far worse than the situation he presently found himself in here on earth. "You had better stay around and find God's solution for your dilemma!" he was kindly admonished.

SUICIDE AND SANITY

At one time it was thought that everyone who committed suicide was mentally deranged, but that has been disproved. What is known, however, is that the person attempting suicide is always desperate—one who has lost all hope.

What is missing? *Hope.*

An individual making a suicide attempt may not be totally mentally deranged, but at the very moment he commits the act of killing himself he is acting out of sheer desperation. Life has lost its meaning; the situation in which he finds himself appears hopeless. Death becomes an emergency exit that frees him from facing the immediate present and the inevitable tomorrow with its pain and problems.

THE 3 H's

Dr. Calvin J. Frederick, psychologist with the National Institute of Mental Health's Center for Studies of Crime and Delinquency, explains the generalized cause of suicide this way: "Usually, people commit suicide because they are hapless, helpless, and hopeless. Hapless, the person feels the cards are stacked against him along with 'tough luck' events. He is lonely and feels helpless to do anything about his situation, and about that time he begins to lose all hope and he is then likely to kill himself." [4]

In trying to pinpoint reasons for suicide, an obvious problem exists—you don't have the victim to talk to. The Los Angeles Institute for the Study of Self-Destructive Behavior, which opened in 1958 as the nation's first suicide-prevention center, conducts what they call "psychological autopsies" to establish whether death was accidental or suicidal. In their efforts to develop a better picture of what drives people to kill themselves, they interview family, friends and other associates of the victim to determine his mental state or attitudes prior to death.

These researchers are also involved in interviewing "failed suicides" in order to develop a better picture of what drives people to make the attempt to kill themselves.

REASONS

Gathering up the statistics and available data, you are struck by one thing—the common thread is the air of hopelessness surrounding the victim's life. This hopelessness is usually manifested by depression. A typical suicide letter will state:

"At this point I've reached an all-time low in my life. My creative drives, ambitions, and human friendliness have seemingly evaporated. I've never felt so alone in my entire life. I feel as though I haven't one friend in the world. I know I'm giving in to self-pitying despair. But I feel so helpless in this hopeless situation. What can I do? I'm at the end of my rope."

Such depression, it can be seen, is the response to a life situation that is perceived as hopeless. One can see the feelings of incompetence, helplessness, lack of resources, of no paths seemingly open. There are guilt feelings, repressed rage, sadness, and unanswered questions as the person gropes his way through the lonely abyss of dark pessimism that can only end in deeper depression and frequently ends in suicide.

Hopelessness also means that the victim has stopped seeking solutions to his or her problems. Death appears as the only way out. J. Wallace Hamilton, in his book, *What About Tomorrow*, makes the observation that in the absence of hope, faith flounders. Hamilton was referring more specifically to a religious faith, but in its broader terms, it could include faith in one's friends, relatives, one's husband or wife, and even one's job. Stress in interpersonal relationships leading to loneliness, alienation or isolation from others, is one of the leading factors contributing to suicide.

These interpersonal difficulties are usually the result of real or imagined failure—another common cause given by those who knew a suicide victim. There may be a long record of failure on jobs and in work relationships. Marital difficulties frequently lead a man or a woman to resort to suicide. The failure to have a harmonious and happy relationship leads one spouse to cop out, and in desperation, attempt suicide.

The loneliness created by a bad marriage cannot be fully appreciated by those who have not been there. On the surface, many marriages may give every appearance of being ideal relationships; yet, far too often, such marriages are only a charade enacted for the public eye. In many such instances there is infidelity on the part of one or the other. The shame and heartache this imposes on the other is frankly beyond description. Suicide often takes its toll from such as these.

Failure can wear a thousand faces. Failure is no respecter of persons and snares many an unsuspecting victim. The result is a bankruptcy of spirit, the consequences of which often lead to suicide.

For women, failure looms as a loss of one's beauty and charm. She cannot cope with the realities of getting older. If her marriage is already suffering, or her dreams have not materialized, she may seek a permanent out. The empty nest syndrome is another factor. This leaves a woman, who has expended herself on her family, feeling that she is no longer needed. The relationship between husband and wife has frequently taken second place while one or the other, or both, centered their interests and attention on the children. Suddenly the children are gone and something is missing.

Student suicides have sharply increased in recent years. Wisdom that comes with maturity is often lacking. School pressure, poor grades, a failed exam, disappointment in friends, these and other factors contribute to the sense of failure a young person may experience.

It is known that scholastic anxiety will trigger the suicide crisis. A terrifying concern of many students is their inability to compete successfully in school. Failure will bring not only disappointment and disapproval from one's parents, but also a shattering of one's own personal confidence. Peer pressure and "What will Joe (or Mary) think," is a contributing factor. Those who knew the suicide victim often use these words: "He pushed himself too hard;" "She worried over her grades;" "He felt his marks weren't as good as they should be." [5]

One student, suffering from such feelings, sent to the *Hollywood Free Paper* office a letter that unmistakably shows this terror even in the writer's scrawl, which fluctuates from normal writing to giant-sized scribbled words where she cries out, "PLEASE HELP!" She accurately describes herself as "a nervous wreck" and again her writing becomes odd-sized, as her frenzy shows through. She then tells of borrowing a boy's pocketknife at school, running out of the building, and "slowly but surely cutting my wrist, but a friend stopped me and got me home in time."

In 1972, suicide ranked third as the cause of death among the general adolescent population. For young people from ages fifteen to nineteen, the suicide rate was 5.5 per 100,000 for boys and 2 per 100,000 for girls. Among collegians the rate was even higher; for every 10,000 college students, 5 to 20 attempted suicide and 1 to 3 succeeded. At that time, suicide was the second most frequent cause of death for collegians, surpassed only by accidents. Today, the phenomenal increase in suicides has placed suicide as the number two cause of death among *all* young people in the 15-24 age group, with accidents as the number one cause. These are young people who don't believe in the future. Obviously, for them, something was missing.

There are many other reasons given as possible causes of suicide—chronic depression, serious illness, job reversals, hysteria, guilt feelings, excessive use of barbituates, postalcoholic withdrawal, old age and the multitudinous problems of the elderly, frustrations, disappointments, racial reasons—all giving stark evidence that life is heaping more on people than they think they can stand. Tired of stumbling over the debris of broken dreams and unfulfilled plans, life has become a long, grim race, and these people don't feel up to staying in the running.

I would hope that there will be those reading this who are suicide failures. You've tried and you've failed. Thank God you failed. Actually, when you set out to write a book you should have an audience in mind. This book is written with suicide failures in mind. It is also our hope that it will be helpful to the 90% of the population who have considered suicide at one time or another.

Those who work with suicidal individuals at suicide prevention centers, and in the mental health profession, state that few suicidal persons will listen closely to any debates about possible causes for suicide or read materials directed at helping them. Most of these deeply troubled men, women, and children are submerged in their own despair. While this is a substantiated fact, I am counting nevertheless on the belief that would-be suicides and failed suicides are still hanging on, as it were, by their fingertips as they search for answers and help. I have received too many letters and counseled with too many people to remain indifferent to these cries for help. Justice Benjamin Cardozo has stated, ''A cry for help is a summons for rescue.'' That is a cry I refuse to ignore.

I have also written this for family members and friends who

have lost loved ones through the act of suicide. *Suicide* is the whispered word. Rarely does it make appropriate dinner time table conversation. It is a taboo topic. After all, who wants to talk about suicide! But surviving members of the family and those who knew the victim need support at this crisis time in *their* lives. For too long society has attempted to ignore the suicide problem as if it didn't exist when, in fact, it is growing in alarming proportions. Most of us prefer to think of suicide as something that happens to other people, but as we separate fact from fiction we discover statistics that bring the tragedy frighteningly close to home. The American Association of Suicidology estimates the annual death toll by suicide at 35,000 in 1977, but nine times that many are said to attempt suicide and survive.

However you look at it, whomever it affects—victims and those left behind who sit and wonder, blaming others and themselves—suicide is tragic and senseless for all concerned.

1. Earl A. Grollman, *Suicide* (Boston: Beacon Press, 1971), p. 93.

2. Dr. Maurice Rawlings, *Beyond Death's Door* (Nashville, Tenn.: Thomas Nelson Publishers, 1978), p. 19.

3. Ibid., p.20.

4. "Upsurge in Suicides and In Ways To Prevent Them," *U.S. News and World Report* (July 1, 1974), p. 48.

5. Grollman, p. 52.

Life is a battle in which we fall
from the wounds we receive in running away.
John Rannell

Women and Suicide

Linda (not her real name) lives alone in a large southern city. Linda is blind. She is a failed suicide. She failed not once, nor twice, but three times in trying to kill herself. Her story is doubly tragic in that on her third suicide try, Linda only succeeded in blinding herself. She should be dead, but she's alive and seeing now in a way she never saw before.

The real tragedy is that this intelligent woman was so bound by her fears, so enslaved to her emotions, and so intent on slashing her way through the jungle called life, that she failed to see what was missing in her life *before* she tried to take it.

Her marriage was a mistake from the beginning. She suffered at the hands of an abusive husband who mistreated not only her, but their children as they came along. You question that we should call a woman who would endure all that *intelligent?* Yet Linda is one of the most intelligent women we have ever met. Her discernment is penetrating; her analysis of situations—both current and what has transpired in the past—is keen. She knows where she's come from and she knows where she's going. Blindness is no deterrent; the difference now is that she no longer forges ahead with her nose leading, swinging her arms frantically to push the underbrush out of the way.

The years of walking on eggshells, living a lie, not confiding in others and living under constant stress in an agony of uncertainty, finally took their toll. Because of two previous suicide attempts, certain family members and so-called friends had Linda believing she was so emotionally disturbed that she was beyond help and hope. Six weeks after a hysterectomy, Linda experienced some physical problems that caused her great anxiety. ''I sat in the doctor's office awaiting my turn. I remember thinking this time my physical problems might lead to death. I was making my children live such a tragic life; they had already suffered enough. What if I had a long lingering time of it? Surely they could adjust to a quick death much easier. With that thought I got up and left the office. I knew what I was going to do. I said nothing to anyone. I just left without a word.''

Linda was raised in a devout Christian home. Her own experience with God was real. By the standards of others, she would have been considered very zealous in her religious beliefs. She continues her story: ''I went home and I remember thinking, God said we had to bear nothing we could not bear. I could not bear to see my kids suffer anymore and since I'd never had an illness unto death, I'd take care of that. The house was in order and I dressed in a dress that I liked very much so I felt ready to go. I got the gun out and then decided to take two sleeping pills so it wouldn't hurt so much in case it wasn't instant. I went to the bedroom and lay down. I picked up the gun and held it to my temple . . .''

After she pulled the trigger she didn't die; she didn't even lose consciousness. ''I thought, 'God, damn you, You will not even let me die. Now what?' The telephone kept ringing and ringing. I thought it would never quit. I didn't answer it. God and I were having a silent argument and I remember thinking, 'Well, at least You are talking to me even if it is to say You are going to have Your way.' The telephone kept ringing. Would it ever stop? At last it did. There was still a very silent struggle going on within me. I would not give up without a battle. But neither would I call for help. I had pulled the trigger at 2 P.M. When I finally did call a friend, I learned it was five hours later. The telephone was in the living room and I do not remember seeing then, but neither do I remember thinking that I could not see. I groped my way to the phone, and then to the door and unlocked it so my friend could get in. Then I returned to the bedroom . . .''

There followed a long stay in the hospital where she underwent neurological and psychological testing. ''I saw two psychiatrists.

Understandably, my anxiety through all of this was great. There was also functional testing which indicated loss of some control in the use of my fingers." The testing itself, however, was preparation for Linda's inner healing and recovery of self-esteem. It was discovered that Linda had unusual insight into people and that her perceptions were accurate. She was not considered psycho. "It is hard to express the feelings of relief," Linda explains. "Now I knew without a doubt that I was of a sound mind. With the Lord's help I had been able to withstand the onslaughts of 'friends' and family members who did not comprehend. God saw me through this crisis experience. I knew from that time on that my strength lay in the Lord. I was released as mentally healthy and completely competent. The Lord blessed me with good medical doctors—men of integrity and thoughtfulness. It had always been easier for me to face concrete obstacles rather than unknown ones; but now I could also face the unknown without despair or resentment. My healing was complete even though I would remain blind."

Subsequent to her suicide attempts, Linda's divorce became final. It is a shared view by psychiatrists that for "divorced and discarded women, suicide serves as an effort to thwart loss of love by a husband or lover. This threatened or actual loss of love awakens infantile and childhood anxiety with resultant feelings of hopelessness, guilt, and rage." Linda fit the pattern common to the divorced women Dr. Albert H. Schrut, Assistant Clinical Professor of Psychiatry, University of Southern California School of Medicine, noted in his study of nine suicidal divorced women. Suicide seeds were planted in these women years before the specific stimulus of a severed relationship. Said Dr. Schrut [*Intellect* magazine, March, 1976), "In many people, the dynamics of suicide stem from early childhood, when the foundation is laid for feelings about oneself. All of the women studied saw themselves as victims of an unjust, severely distant, and deprived childhood. In their relationships with their parents, they suffered feelings of isolation, condemnation, and abandonment. Early in their lives, they acquired feelings of unworthiness and guilt for not fulfilling whatever their parents wanted of them. They felt frustrated, helpless, longing but unable to express their distress." [1]

Linda saw herself as deficient both in the eyes of her parents and her husband, and the thought of adding to the problems of her children tipped the scale. Dr. Schrut explained that the adult life of these suicidal women became an attempt to adapt to or compensate for these "deficiencies." The relationship with men became "obsessive, self-destructive, masochistic, and often sadistic. Divorce or abandonment, of course, resulted."

FEMALE SUICIDES INCREASE

The increase in female suicides has caused, in recent years, the sociologists and other mental-health professionals some puzzlement as to the reasons why. Up until 1960 suicide was, for the most part, a male problem. At that time the ratio of male to female suicides was three to one. Between 1963 and 1976, the national suicide rate for women has gone up by 45 percent. In Los Angeles, the rate of suicide among women in the 15-to-30 age groups increased over 600 percent!

Now it is not at all unusual to pick up the newspaper or a national magazine and read of attempted or completed suicides by women. A California State Department of Public Health report reveals that the stress and strains of "liberation" and work are driving more California women to suicide. Nancy W. Allen, author of the report states: "Women are becoming more involved outside the family and are increasingly entering the working arena . . . Their drive for success and recognition has increased pressures and opened more possibilities for failure . . . In precisely those arenas where liberated women are making most progress, the male-female suicide ratio moves toward 'equality' " (McCall's, January, 1976).

But it is not only the women working outside the home who make suicide attempts. According to Earl Grollman, long involved in family counseling in the state of Massachussetts, the bored housewife has the greatest suicidal potential. A woman approaches marriage with high expectations—expectations unfortunately that are all too often dashed on the cutting edges of the realities that accompany the marriage relationship. It is not all romantic evenings with candlelight dinners for two. Many young couples approach marriage totally unprepared for the inevitable problems which do arise. Every suicide has its own history, of course, but the disillusionment that shatters the dreams of many women comes at the point of marriage adjustments.

One such young woman, hovering on the brink of a suicide attempt, wrote her younger brother a heartwrenching letter:

It's been pretty hilly for me—there have been some valleys I've had to climb out of. Some of those valleys I tried to climb out of by myself but I put my foot in the wrong place and fell back again further than where I was before . . .

Things are somewhat better now, and I shouldn't be writing a letter when I'm down; the trouble is I'm down most of the time and I know you are expecting a letter.

Steve (not his real name) has me worried. Three nights last week he stayed out until after midnight . . . Somehow I muddled through last week but my memory of what happened is just a blur of hurt and frustration. Now it's like a bad dream . . . but I know it was real. Too real . . .

Steve doesn't know what he wants; he doesn't even know if he wants me. He doesn't like the responsibility that goes with marriage. I can't pressure him because then he screams ''freedom!'' He resents the fact that I have a relationship with God. He's turned his back on God. That's not going over too well with God!

At times when I'm able to think straight, I can see what the Lord is doing and a real peace comes over me. I honestly think I would have committed suicide by now if I didn't have the Lord to hold me up.

It's like when the Lord sees a wave coming my way, He lifts me up above it, just high enough so I still get wet enough to learn and to show me how blessed I really am that I didn't go all the way under.

When I look down, it's like I see Steve gasping for air and struggling, fighting all the way—and the whole time all he has to do is stop fighting and reach up for the Lord to pull him up too. Someday he may not be able to fight the wave hard enough and he may not come up again—then it will take an act of grace and mercy for the Lord to reach down and give him one more chance . . .

I've heard and read stories of other women who have gone through what I'm going through. I never thought I'd have to go through it though. Let me tell you, I'm learning a lot.

Mostly I'm learning to just hang in there and to pray. I know I can't change things on my own. I keep praying and ask

God to give me strength and patience in my dealings with Steve. The last time I prayed that, it was though I heard Him say, ''You're doing fine . . .'' That's neat, you know. I think I'm blowing it, but God says I'm doing fine. What would I do without God?''

Another young wife tells of repeatedly hitting her head against the wall in their bedroom in a vain attempt to injure herself so that she would die.

Still another has shared her frequent desire to get in the car and head for a certain section of the highway where there is a bridge abutment. ''It would be so easy to speed up . . .'' she said, sad eyes betraying her pain as her voice trailed off.

Mademoiselle magazine (December, 1972) carried an incisive article entitled ''Suicide and Women'' in which the writer questions why the suicide rate among young women is going up. ''Is there any way to take hold of the increase as a fact, to find some sort of explanation that includes the particular causes?'' The theory is offered that no one can better understand the poverty, isolation and hopelessness that surrounds the elderly, but what is it that invades the lives of the young to cause them to respond with such strong desire to die? This failure of the will to live is an indescribably overwhelming force that should not exist in the lives of those who really have so much for which to live.

It has been demonstrated that a certain area of the will functions in any suicide and these deep pits of melancholy paralyze to such a degree that the resolution necessary for self-destruction is, in the final analysis, lacking for many.

DYING FOR LOVE

Fear of rejection plays an important role in the agony of uncertainty young women experience as they see their husbands struggle with the frustrations that accompany the responsibilities of marriage and the maintenance of a home. Not only is this true for young married women, the same anxiety exists among women who have been married for years. ''Many are skeptical about the notion of dying for love, but love is at the heart of suicide and at the very worst it is a loss of self-love that prompts it. But to lose a love and to be inconsolable are real emotions.'' [2]

In the final analysis, the mystery surrounding motive and mood remains shrouded in the death act itself. What we do know is that traditionally, women make more *attempts* at suicide than men, accounting for eight out of every ten suicide tries. But still men have always outnumbered women in actual deaths by suicide. What does this indicate?

WOMEN DIFFER FROM MEN

There are those who believe women are less sincere in their suicide attempts, i.e., that their attempts are more attention-getters than anything else. Monica Dickens, head of the Boston branch of The Samaritans (a London-originated suicide-prevention center), states: "Most women do not really want to die at all. They are not seriously thinking about being dead. They look on a suicide attempt as a release, an escape from pain." [3]

Women are also prone to look upon suicide as the right thing to do—to sacrifice themselves to spare their loved ones future problems and further anguish. This was seen in Linda's desire to spare her children any more suffering. The great novelist Virginia Woolf left letters to her husband and sister, saying in the suicide's characteristic way, "I can't go on spoiling your life any longer." These women cast their suicide in a heroic mold—that's the way they want to be remembered. Women are more inclined to do that sort of thing than men. That statement is not meant to demean women, but is a recognition of the emotional nature of the female.

Because the scenario of the ultimate desperation is scripted by each individual, it is unsafe to make generalizations about suicide victims. Many complex factors enter into the victim's decision. We know that recurrent depression which frequently triggers suicide can have a biochemical basis; we learn that family histories show a predisposition to suicide. Causes of despondency which precipitate suicide are tangled. Conviction on the part of the victim that his or her circumstances are unalterable will drive them to the act. There are suicides with revenge as the motive—women kill themselves for that reason more frequently than men. Personal anguish and the shame that accompanies the loss of love are more than many women can bear. To know that one's husband or lover has left you for someone else is devastating. Life is for living, but the effort is too great.

Women look at their offspring and see failure—failure in themselves as mothers. They know that others see the failure also. Self-hatred, self-accusation and their limitations rise up to stare them in the face. It is intolerable. They cannot face the critical analyses of self nor the condemning finger of others. How should they deal with it?

Methods of suicide seem to vary by gender with women selecting more passive means of killing themselves—sleeping pills, poisons, slit wrists, or gas. Women want to look their best in death, so they usually don't attempt to blow out their brains or do something that would disfigure themselves in some way. Linda was an exception with her choice of a gun, but note her concern about wearing the right dress.

Women want the painless way out (Linda took sleeping pills in case she didn't die right away). The easy availability of potentially dangerous drugs is offered as a factor in the increase in women's suicide rates. It is known that twice as many women as men, notably in the 20-to-40-year-old age bracket, are now on tranquilizers and other forms of psychotropic drugs. In the course of writing this. I received a phone call from a woman telling me she had flushed all her Valium down the toilet while on vacation. "It was tempting me; I was despondent and the future looked so bleak. I knew if I kept those pills around I might take all of them without really meaning to. I do want to live, but it's just that I can't see the end from the beginning. Is there any hope?"

The 1976 statistics reveal that 50,000 people (reportedly—who can know the actual number?) died of tranquilizer overdoses, and 250,000 more received emergency medical attention for drug overdoses. The majority of these, however, are not listed as suicides or suicide attempts. Out of these two groups, two-thirds were women.

Before leaving the subject of women and suicide, something else must be emphasized. Let there be a recognition that among suicide victims, we are seeing a dramatic increase in completed suicide by professional women. These are women who have achieved success in their chosen profession—medicine, psychology, writing, teaching, the arts, etc . . . Psychoanalysts and authors like Dr. Robert Seidenberg offer some helpful insights as to the why behind this new phenomenon. "This is the first decade that women have been massively educated and sent out into the world. But sooner or later they realize that they are still largely unwanted. Men still don't really want women for expertise, for leadership, for decision making. And if you think it is bad to be an unwanted child, it is doubly bad to feel like an unwanted adult." [4]

Another strong factor which enters the scene relates to the need for women to act decisively in their job roles. Translate that learned ability to act and to make decisions and stick to them in their professions into the other end of the emotional scale as it relates to themselves as women, and you can see the problem this poses when they are confronted with personal trauma. Traditionally women have been ambivalent in hysterical attempts to do away with themselves (just enough sleeping pills to put themselves out for hours, making sure they hinted to someone so they would be found in time); an indulgence many females have resorted to. But now we are seeing more completed suicides, a result, it is believed, of the need for women to make decisions and not waver in carrying them out—even suicide.

Someone wrote to Ann Landers with a warning: Prospective Suicides: Think of Those You'll Hurt. The letter stated:

DEAR ANN LANDERS: I am a fairly attractive woman in my middle forties. To the outside world I appear to have everything a woman could want—a lovely home, beautiful children, a successful husband, and I've even excelled in sports and have won some trophies. No one would suspect that I've gone through periods of severe depression and about two years ago attempted suicide.

I have something important to say to the readers of your column who may have at any time contemplated taking their lives. The information I am about to pass along for free, cost me $3,000 in psychiatric bills.

The next time you look longingly at that handgun, or that bottle of pills, or a bridge or window you believe will put an end to your agonies, remember the husband or wife or children or parents you would leave behind. No matter how blameless they may be, they will always think it was their fault that you killed yourself. All the rationalization in the world won't change it. They will carry to their graves the thought that something they did, or failed to do, caused you to take your life.

Do you want to place such a burden on your loved ones? If you commit suicide you'll surely do it—Thank God I Didn't.

DEAR FRIEND: The impact of any given letter is, of

course, an unknown quantity, but I can tell you for certain that your letter prevented at least one suicide someplace in the world today. Thank your for writing it. [5]

1. "Suicide Wish Among Divorcees," *Intellect* (March, 1976), p. 418.

2. "Suicide and Women," by Elizabeth Hardwick, *Mademoiselle* (December, 1972), p. 159.

3. "Why Women Are Committing Suicide," Cimi Star and Sheri Steiner, *McCalls* (January, 1976), p. 47.

4. Ibid., p. 47.

5. "Prospective Suicides: Think of Those You'll Hurt," by Ann Landers, *Daily News Tribune* (June 8, 1974), p. A-4.

> Anyone who has sat by the bedside
> of a patient dying from a self-inflicted
> wound and listened to pleadings that
> the physician save his life, the
> destruction of which had only a few
> hours or minutes before been attempted,
> must be impressed by the paradox
> that one who has wished to kill
> himself does not wish to die!
> Dr. Karl Menninger [1]

4

Sad, Young and Wanting to Die

"I was eleven years old. Life was just so pathetically empty. I remember taking a bottle of medicine I found in the medicine cabinet. I knew it was poisonous because it had a skull and crossbones on it. When no one was looking, I mixed it with peanut butter and spread it on a piece of bread. Then I ate it, went upstairs and crawled in bed.

"Later, I awoke and was disappointed that I wasn't dead. I really didn't even feel very sick (I guess I didn't get enough from one piece of bread). Still later I was glad I hadn't died. I couldn't understand myself—one day wanting to be dead, the next day glad to be alive even though our circumstances hadn't changed. I wondered then if life was always going to be that way.

"My parents were terribly religious in a frightening sort of way—always talking about God coming to destroy the world and taking the good people away first. I didn't think a God who did that could be very nice. For a long time I spent endless hours trying to dig a big tunnel I could run to and escape from that kind of a God when He came. I finally gave up on that project.

"I gave up on God about then, too.

"But I didn't give up the idea of killing myself. I always held it out to myself as a last resort. Sort of a 'Well, kid, you know you can always kill yourself when things get too bad.' "

"I sat there listening to my hairdresser, having taken time out on a trip to have some work done on my hair. She had a small, black book lying on the counter. In bright red letters I read: SUICIDE. When I questioned her about the book and her interest in the subject of suicide she shared with me how she had made four attempts to take her own life. Each, obviously, had failed.

"How old are you now?" I questioned.

"Shamefully, she glanced down, then looked at me in the mirror. 'I'm only twenty-three,' she replied.

"And so we talked. We talked of suicide and being sad and young and wanting to die. God certainly makes no mistakes. Under the dryer I silently thanked Him for having me cancel a previous appointment at another hotel a few blocks away, and on an impulse checking in at the other place instead.

"As we talked, I learned that it was the help she received at a Teen Challenge Center that finally checked the suicide impulses and resulted in her life getting straightened out. But she still had some questions and so we talked at length. "I know now that I'll never try suicide again," she related. 'I've been getting answers to my questions in surprising ways—like today,' and she smiled."

BRIDGES OF LOVE

Those who work with failed suicides have made the discovery that usually a suicidal episode occurs in the form of a crisis of limited duration. How important it is that each of us be "bridges of love," as it were, to those with whom we come in contact. You never know what your smile, your cheery "Hello, how are you?" and your kindness—even to a total stranger—may mean to that individual at that particular juncture in his life. Of particular importance, of course, is the need for family members to communicate love to one another in both big and little ways.

Suicide prevention centers and the organized efforts of society to decrease the number of suicides are doing much to communicate to the lonely, the disenchanted, the depressed, and the alienated. But in a very real way each of us can serve as a suicidal prevention center by communicating love and understanding.

On the whole, society is simply too busy, too indifferent, and really quite callous. We actually live quite an isolated existence, even in our more densely populated urban areas. This was strikingly shown—in a calamitous example of human isolation—in the suicide death of a college student found in his room after he had been dead eighteen days! There were no friends, no one involved enough in his life to know or to care that he had been missing for more than two weeks.

What tragedy! How this tears at one's heart! Yet at an age when they supposedly have everything to live for, almost five thousand teenagers and young adults each year—about thirteen a day—are so trapped in despair that they commit suicide.

But these statistics don't even reflect the full problem. It's a recognized fact that not every suicide is reported as such. The resulting stigma for remaining family members is too great and so efforts are made to conceal the fact that many untimely deaths are, in fact, suicides. And it is known that for every suicide by a young person there are many more attempts—some think as many as fifty per day.

Dr. Calvin Frederick of the National Institute of Mental Health was quoted in the newspapers (The *Sacramento Bee*, July 20, 1978) as stating: "It is a striking phenomenon and tragic because they haven't had a chance to start to live."

CAUSES IN YOUTH SUICIDES

Frederick believes that suicidal young persons often have ineffectual father-son, mother-daughter relationships and often suffer great pressure by trying to live up to parental expectations.

He cites breakdown of the family, increased use of drugs and alcohol and the difficulty of getting a job and getting ahead as factors.

"The cards seemed stacked against them, everything turns out badly, they don't have the resources to lift themselves up and then they lose hope. That is a suicidal combination," Frederick said.

The lack of communication that exists between parents and children is a frightening reality. One statistic that leaves you gasping in horror reveals that eighty-eight percent of youthful suicide occurred at home, very often with parents in the next room!

Several factors present themselves:

- Parents are too busy, too preoccupied with their own lives to pay enough attention to their children, particularly when they become teenagers.
- When parents are with their children they fail to listen to what their offspring are saying; they make little or no effort to try and

comprehend what the young person is *really* saying and thinking.

- Too many parents are substituting their authority for honest answers to their children's questions.
- Parents have set bad examples for their children in their own use of drugs and alcohol.
- Parental fighting with the threat of divorce looming always in the background has caused young people to feel frightened, upset and insecure.
- Parents do not know their children's friends.
- Parents have failed in providing the right set of values.
- Parents have not established religious moorings nor helped their children understand the need for a relationship with their Creator and development of a faith that sustains in times of trouble.
- Parents are not home when children need them; this is complicated by the fact that in so many homes both parents are working.

Parade magazine asked Dr. Joseph D. Teicher, of the University of Southern California School of Medicine, what brings a teenager to the point of hopelessness. He responded by saying the adolescent believes that death is the final solution after he has failed in all other attempts to cope with his problems.

Dr. Teicher went on to explain: "Although a first suicide attempt always comes as a surprise to parents and friends of the attempter, it can never be dismissed as an impulsive act, the result of a temporary upset. In most cases, the teenager considers the suicide in advance, weighing it against other alternatives." [2]

This same magazine article gives results of research at the Los Angeles County USC Medical Center which reveals that involvement in the following situations and circumstances preceded the adolescents' suicide attempt:

(1) 40 percent had a parent, relative, or close friend who attempted suicide.

(2) 72 percent had one or both natural parents absent from home because of divorce, separation, or death.

(3) 84 percent of those with stepparents felt they were contending with an unwanted stepparent.

(4) 58 percent had a parent who was married more than once.

(5) 15 percent had serious problems because of at least one parent's alcoholism.

(6) 62 percent had both parents working or one working when there was only one parent in the family.

(7) A large percentage lived with persons other than their parents. [3]

SUICIDE AS PROTEST

Young people are not immune from feeling a concern about the state of the nation and the world. Spectators and graduates in Weymouth South High School, Weymouth, Massachusetts watched in horror as seventeen-year-old Karim Thompson stepped to the microphone at his high school graduation in 1978 and said, "This is the American way," and shot himself. Ironically, this occurred after the young man and other members of the school's choral group had finished singing "Teach Your Children."

The local police investigator, who saw the shooting on the school's athletic field, rushed to the platform where the young man lay on the ground, clutching a .22-caliber revolver, and heard Karim say, "There are too many issues in America today" (*The Atlanta Constitution*, June 12, 1978).

In a world that is becoming increasingly depersonalized, superficial and artificial, suicide seems far more desirable than does living a life of pretense in hopelessness. This was shown in the despair that preceded and prompted the death by suicide of two young people, seventeen-year-old versions of the all-American dream, as told in the book *Craig and Joan: Two Lives for Peace:* [4] This is the tragic but true story of two bright, popular students who died on October 15, 1969, their lives sucked out of their bodies by a vacuum cleaner hose attached to the car exhaust. It is a distressing story of pain, love, and terror, but the book dramatically points up the high ideals, dreams and hopes of young people today living in a society that is becoming increasingly complex.

Craig and Joan were not drug addicts or morally depraved individuals. They did everything in the power of a teenaged cheerleader and an intelligent teenaged young fellow to convince those they knew and loved of the importance of right living. They were both deeply concerned about war. Death seemed to be the best way to have an impact on people's thinking, to be convincing. They left behind twenty-four notes of explanation and desire, but only two of them were ever printed.

What Craig and Joan apparently failed to realize is that they didn't have to make that kind of sacrifice—their own lives—that Someone had preceded them in sacrificing His life. The story can be found in the Gospel of Matthew (chapter 20, verse 28) in the Bible.

We live in a world where there will be constant strife, war, and an absence of peace. Taking one's own life in protest for the inequities of life isn't going to alter the situation. It may produce a disturbing and unsettling effect on those closest to the one or ones who may do as Craig and Joan did, and it may even have a rippling effect on others elsewhere, but the long-range effect is not worthy of such a terrible and senseless sacrifice of life.

Young people who have been given too much and who have not been trained to accept responsibility are prime candidates for suicide. With their values askew, they play with their $40,000 "toys"—their hand-built cars—and make statements like this: "If they (the police) caught me (speeding) they'd impound my car and mess it up. I'd kill myself if anything happened to this car. I love it more than anything." [5]

In stark contrast to the child who seemingly has everything is the story of the fourteen-year-old boy, jailed for truancy, who hung himself in a Conroe, Texas jail. The mother said of his death, "I don't know whether I should start blaming people or just sit down and wonder" (Los Angeles *Times*, November, 1971).

MIXED FEELINGS

A young boy's letter shows the ambivalent feelings the suicidal person has:

> "A friend and I decided to end it all and so we went into a drugstore and ripped off two boxes of car sickness pills. Life seemed so empty. Then we went into the bathroom of a service station, we could hardly walk and saw horrible things all night long. We were half out of our minds and then my friend started screaming for me to call an ambulance. He just about died at the hospital and then started praying to God not to let him die."

One moment, the person is certain that he wants to die; a short while later he is convinced that if he can just hold on a while longer, life is worth living. Sigmund Freud, founder of psychoanalysis, authored the earliest psychological explanation of suicide, in which he shows this contradiction in life of self-preservation and self-destructiveness. There are basically two strong drives in one's life: the life instinct, or Eros; and the death, destructive, and aggressive drive, or Thanatos. Freud explained suicide as aggression turned upon the self, whereas murder is aggression turned upon another. Thus, suicide becomes murder in the 180th degree. Both suicide and murder are aspects of Thanatos. [6]

A great profusion of material has been amassed dealing with suicidal behavior. The U.S. Public Health Service has an up-to-date bibliography showing the contributions that have been made in such findings and literature. Local suicide prevention centers, the National Institute of Mental Health, local libraries, and books that can be found in bookstores will contribute material for anyone who wishes to pursue the study of suicidal behavior and its prevention in more detail.

From the accumulated mass of information it can definitely be stated that distress, despair, unhappiness, poor interpersonal relationships, social disorganization, and adverse early (childhood) experiences are all notable features of attempted or completed suicides. Self-destruction is not a theological issue; Grollman says and we agree, it is the result of unbearable emotional stress. [7]

There are all sorts of variables and precipitating factors, but those who attempt suicide are people whose lives are most frequently characterized by social and psychological deficits that pose several problems for them, their family members, and those who attempt to help and treat them. The suicidal person is suffering from what has been described as ''tunnel vision''—that is, a limited focus, with his mind unable to furnish him with a complete picture of how to handle his seemingly intolerable problems.

1. Karl A. Menninger, *Man Against Himself*, (New York: Harcourt, Brace, 1938).

2. ''Teen-Age Suicide Rise,'' *Parade* (January 28, 1973).

3. Ibid.

4. Eliot Asinof, *Craig and Joan: Two Lives for Peace* (New York: Viking Press, 1971).

5. David Barry, ''Thunder Road,'' *New West* (July 31, 1978), p. 37.

6. Sigmund Freud, *Civilization and Its Discontents* (New York: Norton, 1962); and ''Morning and Melancholia,'' *Collected Papers*, Volume II (London: The Hogarth Press, 1949).

7. Earl A. Grollman, *Suicide* (Boston: Beacon Press, 1971), p. 88.

"I wish I could tell Mother how torn I
am—like two people pulling me apart.
The Good One and the Bad One, and I'm
going to die in the middle."
An unidentified child who
failed in a suicide attempt. [1]

5

The Child Suicides:
Death Before Life

They swallow poison.
 Dart into heavy traffic.
  Slash their wrists.
   Beat and disfigure themselves.
    Take medicine and drugs.
     Hang themselves.

                                    In
                                 these
                                  and
                              other
                            grim
                           ways
                          they
      self-destruct—The child suicides.

Death by natural reasons brings with it a gamut of emotions for
those who remain—loneliness, heartache, disbelief. Even when
death is expected because of a lingering illness, or there has been
some time in which to prepare one's self, there is still the
accompanying emotional pain. But death by suicide is a robber.
The emotional reaction of grief-stricken parents, brothers and sis-
ters, grandparents, other relatives, teachers, schoolmates, and
friends is greatly intensified. In addition to the usual emotional
trauma and accompanying adjustment, there are aggravated
feelings of guilt, self-blame, and even shame.

Over and over again, those who knew the suicide victim question, ''What did I do wrong? What didn't I do that I should have done? Could I have prevented this in some way? Were they signaling for my help, and did I fail to respond?''

Earl Grollman states: ''For the family, tragedy is just beginning. There is just not enough time to heal the wounds of a self-inflicted death. The crushing blow is a bitter experience for all those left behind. They carry it in their hearts for the rest of their lives . . . Suicide is the cruelest death of all for those who remain.'' [2]

Up until recent years, suicide among children was comparatively rare. But today we are seeing a frightening increase in child suicides. Latest available figures (1976) show that slightly less than 200 suicides under fourteen years old were recorded. Always, however, when statistics are given, there is the accompanying word: ''But many suicides go unreported, and . . . so-called accidental injuries and poisonings in school-age children are often 'purposeful, self-destructive acts.' '' [3]

Dr. Howard Hansen, head of the division of psychiatry at Children's Hospital of Los Angeles-Edgemont Hospital, reported at a summer (1978) conference on the subject of childhood suicide and depression, that fully one-fourth of the admissions to the psychiatric unit involved children who had made suicide attempts or who had a preoccupation with self-destruction.

For a long time both parents and professionals ignored the possibility that young children could feel pain to such a degree that they would intentionally seek death as a way out. At UCLA's Neuropsychiatric Institute (NPI) they know differently. A four-year study involving thirty-four preteens labeled severely depressed and self-abusive or suicidal turned up surprising findings.

The Los Angeles *Times* reported these findings and the views of three national experts at the Lake Arrowhead conference sponsored by the Southern California Society for Child Psychiatry. Much in this chapter is based on the reporting of that event. [4]

UCLA medical psychologist Morris J. Paulson emphasized that aloneness, fear of rejection and threats of violence are as meaningful to a four-year-old as to an adult. ''Health providers and caregivers must realize that (some) young children are 'at risk' for suicide.''

EMOTIONAL POVERTY

The economic level of the family of suicidal children is not a determining factor, but the emotional poverty found in nearly all the families plays a major role in contributing to the child's wish to die:

- Some of the chidren had close relatives who had also attempted suicide.
- More than half the parents were separated or divorced; the remainder could hardly be said to be living in harmony.
- Perceived or imagined abandonment by a parent figure was the more frequent immediate event leading to referral (to the NPI clinic for treatment).
- Hostile, feuding, pathological relationships of violence between husbands and wives caused feelings of emotional rejection.

Children who have attempted suicide and who were seen at NPI, varied in their methods of ways to self-destruct. But each revealed the symptoms of emotional poverty described. Their actions sound more like something out of a horror movie than real life:

"I would be better off dead," explained a twelve-year-old girl who survived from an overdose of hypnotic drugs. "Then no one would ever have to look at my ugly face again." This child had hung her doll by its neck, drugged her little sister, cut both her legs with scissors and slashed her wrists before overdosing.

"Mother doesn't have any love in her for me," cried an eleven-year-old boy who tried to kill his dog, attempted to suffocate his baby brother with a pillow, and stabbed pins and needles into his stomach.

"A six-year-old boy who wanted to die 'Because nobody loves me,' first cut himself with his father's razor before being rescued from a second-story window where he tried to hang himself."

The inconsolable grief parents experience by a child's suicide, and the accompanying guilt with which they are afterwards tormented, should serve as an example to other parents to work to improve relationships within the family.

Psychologist Morris J. Paulson explains: "The witnessing of family violence both verbal and physical, precipitated acute panic, fear and concern that they (the child) also may be the next victim of violent assault."

One such child, an eight-year-old girl, receiving NPI help, pathetically confided, "They don't like me. I wish I was dead."

Said another: "I would rather die than be spanked. They want me dead."

Feeling emotionally rejected by his mother, one six-year-old sadly expressed his hurt, "I want to die because nobody loves me." This child's mother had decided to go back to work and the child (wrongly) interpreted this as rejection.

Such feelings of rejection are not uncommon when there is the birth of a new brother or sister in a family. The child, who may have low feelings of self-esteem, sees the newcomer as a rival for the parents' love.

CHILD ABUSE

Hardly anything is more sad than to see children abused by adults. Linda's children (Chapter 3) were the victims of their father's terrible temper. In this family situation, it was the mother who made three suicide attempts. But NPI and other such centers and hospital emergency rooms, see battered children who, in sheer desperation, try to take their own lives. Not all are as philosophical as one ten-year-old whose thirteen-year old brother had committed suicide earlier. "Everyone kills and everyone dies . . . there is no escape," the child philosophized in hopeless resignation to his own sad fate.

The Los Angeles *Times*, in reporting these situations discussed at the conference, noted that these children and their parents were treated with a variety of therapies: behavior modification, individual or family psychotherapy; and hospitalization, foster home, institutional placement or adoption were sometimes necessary. Three years later, only thirteen of those thirty-four treated could be traced. But of those, none had committed suicide.

DEPRESSION

Depression is the leading cause of suicide and suicidal behavior, accounting for up to 79 percent of all attempters. [5] Suicide potential may be directly related to the severity of depressive symptoms. [6]

The problem is compounded, however, in diagnosing depression in the very young, because the very young present different features in manifesting their depression, [7] as contrasted to adults.

The psychiatrist who heads the only hospital ward in the United States devoted to studying childhood depression. Dr. Joaquim Puig-Antich of Columbia University and the New York State Psychiatric Institute, estimates that at least one percent of all children are depressed. This is based, in turn, on estimates that ten to fifteen percent of children in urban areas have some psychiatric disorder and that disorder is depression in five percent to ten percent of those cases. [8]

Currently there is controversy among professionals centering on whether children can suffer adult-like psychiatric depression: an illness with definite signs and symptoms, a family history of related disorders, certain biochemical levels in the body and a predictable response to antidepressant drugs.

Dr. Gabrielle Carlson, UCLA psychiatrist, explains that no one denies that children feel sad and discouraged at times, and they will experience depression at being separated from a loved one or at being trapped in a miserable environment. Studies underway by Carlson, Puig-Antich and others should reveal in time whether such children will outgrow this depression or become depressed adults. In the meantime, however, suicide and suicide behavior continues among children. [9]

Dr. Carlson investigated the case histories of fifty manic-depressive patients at the National Institute of Mental Health trying to determine early signs of depression or other psychiatric illnesses in their childhoods. But her reportings revealed few. Manic-depression is characterized by high and low mood swings. This kind of depression doesn't seem to start until adolescence. Dr. Puig-Antich believes, however, that some depressed children may simply start with the lows and not experience the first high (the manic phase of the illness) until the teens. [10]

IS THERE SOME WAY
TO RECOGNIZE A DEPRESSED CHILD?

To try and answer that question poses some problems. It is hoped that readers won't become armchair psychologists pointing their fingers at friends' children or other youngsters and labeling them "depressed."

A generally unhappy mood accompanied by extreme irritableness and weeping would be symptomatic. According to researchers like Carlson and Puig-Antich, other symptoms would include:

- Thoughts of death or suicide.
- Strong verbal clues ("You'd be better off without me").
- Tiredness.
- Withdrawal from other people; a significant change in social behavior.
- Aggressiveness and getting into fights.
- Loss of interest in things that used to be fun; a dramatic shift in daily behavior (boredom, restlessness, preoccupation).
- Guilt feelings.
- Poor concentration (and consequently, poor performance in school).
- Giving away prized possessions.
- Insomnia or sleeping a lot.
- Sometimes a change in appetite and/or weight.

They state that if a child appears sad and has as many as five of these symptoms for more than a couple of weeks, chances are he or she is depressed. [11]

IS IT KNOWN HOW SUCH DEPRESSION DEVELOPS?

According to the Los Angeles *Times* Report, the current view of how depression develops is that depression runs in families. But children born with a susceptibility to this disorder—called a "high genetic load" in scientific parlance—may not become depressed until later in life, if ever. What can trigger this depression would be some traumatic events—separations, divorce, cruelty, neglect, the death of someone close—and this during their first five years.

It doesn't take being a psychologist to understand that the potential for this to happen to children in our kind of society today is astronomical.

Myrna M. Weissman, Assistant Professor in Psychiatry at Yale University School of Medicine, and Director, Depression Research Unit, The Connecticut Mental Health Center, has supplied us with valuable research in her paper reporting findings on "The Epidemiology of Suicide Attempts, 1960 to 1971." [12] What she and other researchers are interested in accomplishing, is, of course, primary prevention methods. Ms. Weissman states: "Primary prevention touches on the fundamental structure of social

and family life . . ." She points to the social disorganization surrounding us today. Such things as geographical mobility which
contributes to social isolation (in the United States increasingly we
are becoming a population on the move)—this means loss of community, familiar friends and family, coupled with the physical
stress of resettling contributes to feelings of anomia ("Nobody
knows me," rootlessness) and alienation in the young.

Weissman suggests the changing roles of women may be yet
another link between the rise in the rate of young suicide attempters and the youth culture of past decades. Her research findings
show that most writers today view our present youth culture as a
recent historical development in an industrial society. The biological age of puberty has decreased because of improvement in
nutrition and health. There have been strains placed upon our
institutions that provide guidance and education for our young.
With the weakness of the nuclear family, and the failure in so
many schools, youth are quick to sense and see this social disorganization. While they couldn't describe it (particularly the very
young), it still has its effect.

Coming back to what Puig-Antich and Carlson have said, we
can see an emerging picture of childhood depression as being the
same illness possibly as suffered by adults, but simply occurring at
a different point in development. The collision of genetic vulner-
ability (depression historically running in the family) and poor
early home environment makes such *Depression* (with a capital
D) predictable.

Pilot studies on thirteen depressed children between six and
twelve years of age (at the Bronx Municipal Hospital Center and
the Sound View-Throggs Neck Community Mental Health Center
in New York), Puig-Antich and other researchers at Albert
Einstein College of Medicine found eleven had suffered major
losses or long separations from parents or other important figures.
And eleven came from families where fighting was a way of life. [13]

These researchers gathered information on eighty-three of these
children's relatives and discovered severe depression or alcoholism in fifty-one.

Carlson's studies at UCLA on twenty-eight depressed youngsters between the ages of seven and seventeen showed that one-
third of them had close relatives who were alcoholics, and half had
depressive or manic-depressive relatives. [14]

A WINDOW ON THE BRAIN

Researchers who work with blood samples of severely depressed children have discovered an excessive amount of cortisol, an essential hormone secreted by the adrenal gland. They tell us that depression appears to be the only disease in which the cortisol "faucet" fails to shut off in the evening as it does in normal people. By measuring these hormone levels, the researchers get a sort of window on the brain. They already know the brain chemicals that are implicated in adult depression. Such depression in adults is regulated by antidepressant drugs through the limbic system which is thought to be the seat of the emotions. The limbic system, in turn, regulates the pituitary which regulates the adrenal gland. Blood samples and testing can provide clues as to what's going on up in the brain.15

Sound confusing? To the untrained mind it may; but to those entrusted with trying to wipe out depression in preventive efforts to minimize suicide and suicidal attempts in children and in young people, it is terribly important. Such men and women, dedicated as they are to their work, are very crucial in the ongoing work that is needed. Who knows? Their work may spell the difference between life and death by suicide for someone dear to you.

1. Mary Susan Miller, "Teen Suicide," *Ladies Home Journal* (February, 1977), pp. 72, 74.

2. Earl A. Grollman, *Suicide* (Boston: Beacon Press, 1971), p. 109.

3. Lois Timnick, "Child Suicides," Los Angeles *Times* (July 25, 1978), Part I, p. 17.

4. Ibid.

5. Myran M. Weissman, "The Epidemiology of Suicide Attempts, 1960 to 1971," New Haven, Conn., *Arch Gen. Psychiatry*/Vol. 30, (June, 1974), p. 741.

6. Ibid.

7. Ibid.

8. Timnick.

9. Ibid.

10. Ibid.

11. Ibid.

12. Weissman.

13. Timnick.

14. Ibid.

> Suicide is an insult to humanity.
> Immanuel Kant

6

Men and Suicide

Ask ten different people if they have ever contemplated suicide and the very reticence of some to reply, provides the clue that they have. During the course of writing this, I questioned a much-respected businessman if he thought a book on this subject was needed. His answer was an immediate *"Yes,"* said in such a way that you surmised there was more to his answer than he was relating. Then he provided more of an answer: "For many years now, I've held out to myself the idea that if things get too tough, I can always kill myself. I know that comes as a shock, but since you asked, I have to be honest. Maybe it will help in the writing of the book; maybe it is a reflection of what lots of men think. If so, we are in trouble. Try and provide us with some reasons and answers as to why we feel that way and what we can do."

Better Homes and Gardens magazine (April, 1977), in an article entitled "Suicide, Let's Separate Fact From Fiction" stated that five million Americans have tried suicide at some time in their lives, and that this constitutes a complete cross section of the population, representing all religions, races, sexes, economic groups, social classes, and personality types. In describing the "most typical" suicide they depict him as being a well-adjusted mainstream American—a male in his 40s, a breadwinner, a family man, a homeowner, and a man whose best years would seem to be ahead of him.

Dr. Norman Farberow (co-director, Los Angeles Suicide Prevention Center), in answering the question "Who commits suicide?" replied: "We've done many psychological autopsies, and it's become clear that the act is not limited to a particular kind of person. The most common characteristics are male, white,

Protestant, age 45 to 60. It's always a person who has encountered problems, most often with his wife, family or other personal relationships, problems that he feels he cannot cope with.'' [1]

FLAMEOUT

It has been pointed out that attempted suicides are higher among women, but completed suicides are higher among men. The ratio of male to female suicides is slightly less than two to one (*Better Homes and Gardens,* April, 1977). This change reflects a rise in suicide among women rather than a decline in suicide among men.

The methods of suicide that men and women choose account, in part, for the fact that more men are successful in completing their suicide act. Women traditionally have chosen ''slow'' methods of death, such as ingestion of poisons and medicines, that increase the chance of rescue. Such a suicide attempt may be interpreted as a way of asking for help, of calling attention to the woman's problems and asking others to be concerned about them. Men, however, often construe asking for help as weak and unmanly. Rather than seeking assistance, they may reach for a gun and act with tragic finality. [2]

It is generally thought that women are more vain than men. This may be true; but men also notice the relentless march that moves them forward toward middle age. There are physiological alterations (appearance and often agility) and accompanying psychological changes. Goals have not been attained and dreams, aspirations, and plans begin to appear as improbable to be realized. Depression sets in—a deep-down, immobilizing despair that saps creative energy and drive. With this comes loss of a will to live. The tragedy is that the wish to die and loss of the will to live is transitory in most instances, and the suicide's depression has temporarily blinded him to other ways out of his dilemma. If family members or business associates were only aware, and if when the person feels suicidal they would reach out and confide in someone and seek some help, all it would take is a word of encouragement and understanding to make such a person become conscious of alternative solutions to his situational difficulty.

Time magazine (June 12, 1972) reported that dentists lead all professions in killing themselves, followed closely by psychiatrists.

Doctors are also killing themselves with increasing frequency

(*Science Digest,* October, 1974). What leads them to this kind of a demise? Dr. Robert E. Litman, Director of the Suicide Prevention Center, Los Angeles, offers the explanation that many physicians cherish the image of invulnerability to illness. "The concept of the medical family as persons made of iron constitutes a barrier to seeking needed treatment. The emphasis on secrecy is increased when the physician's problem is alcoholism, drug abuse or episodes of mania or depression."

Earl Grollman explains the pattern of executive suicide like this: "A rising young executive, aflame with creative ideas, moves through a series of regular promotions. Then in what should be highly productive middle years, he suddenly 'flames out.' " [3]

Grollman quotes Dr. Herbert Klemme, Director of the Division of Industrial Mental Health at the Menninger Foundation. "As a person reaches the crest of life, after age thirty-five or so, he begins to struggle with the inevitability of his own death. He has to revise his life goals in terms of what is still possible to do. He has to be realistic and settle for a little less than he had hoped to achieve. For the person who is not reaching the goals he has set for himself, the effects can be unsettling or even devastating." [4]

We have in this country what has appropriately been labeled a "youth cult." We seem to worship at the "shrine" of youth. Men, who are just coming into their greatest potential in their middle years, are often stripped of position and replaced by someone younger. Suicides increase during these years. A plea to industry and business is in order. When a man has proven himself competent and has been loyal, to deny him future progression in the company merely because the company is looking for "new, young blood" is a cruel recourse that can lead to serious consequences. *Harvard Business Review* (July-August, 1975) urged accurate, honest, and frequent performance appraisals for executives within a company to enable the executive to maintain a perspective on himself.

This magazine article pointed out that everyone needs confirmation from others of his performance. Statistics alone are cold and do not satisfy that need. If the executive is *not* performing well, far better for him to learn about it far enough in advance to do something about it. He may suffer a temporary decline in his self-image, but the appraisal can open up other alternatives to him.

Men in situations like this need to remember that their peers have similar problems.

WHY MEN? WHY?

The rigid self-demands that so many men place upon themselves is neither wise nor fair, neither to themselves, nor to their families. Some self-appraisal is called for. The economic needs of today propel many men into long hours of fatiguing work with accompanying pressures for achievement and approval forced upon them. Husbands and wives need to communicate to each other their values. It is one thing for a man to have high aspirations, but it is another thing to be so driven by the need to fulfill these goals that he excludes his wife and family, and success for success sake becomes the driving motivation. Such a man is a prime target for suicidal thoughts when business reverses rear their ugly heads.

IS DEATH THE ONLY WAY OUT OF DILEMMAS?

British Poet-Critic A. Alvarez, in his book *The Savage God*, regards suicide theory and statistics as, in the final analysis, quite unilluminating. He speaks of the "shabby, confused, agonized crisis which is the common reality of suicide." *Time* magazine (June 12, 1972) suggests that suicide is more like cancer, a mysterious plague that cries out not for philosophy but for a palliative.

In times of recession the suicide rate always rises. But in recent years, we have seen more and more executives reacting to a single defeat in a business setting by becoming suicidal. Generally these are men who have been very successful, as their top-ranking positions indicate, and also men who had strong consciences. To attempt suicide is to act in violation of their consciences. A double tragedy. These are men who are needed in society; these are men whose families will feel the loss deeply.

Harvard Business Review (July, 1975) states: "The conscientious person with high aspirations which he pursues intently is especially vulnerable to setbacks that may lead to depression and even self-destruction."

Oftentimes, the executive who takes his own life, is assumed to be taking the only way out to avoid the intolerable consequences of guilt. Writer Harry Levinson (*Harvard Business Review*) says that conclusion is too glib and that management ranks need to grapple with the special nature of factors which led to the suicide's decision.

When status is destroyed, when self-esteem is shaken to the very core, and the future looms as unpredictable with no solution in sight, a man's perspective gets out of focus. It becomes easy to begin to think irrationally. Researchers tell us if such a person has sustained psychological bruises in childhood, and the loss of love and support (through death, divorce, or separation of parents), he may have developed deeply ingrained habit patterns of ego ideal aspirations. The consequent pressures to achieve these levels of perfection, with the threat of real or imagined failure hovering on the horizon of his thinking, may drive him to attack himself in the form of accidents, or in the extreme, by committing suicide.

This is a form of self-flagellation that is not uncommon. But people can destroy themselves in many other ways. We see this in ruined marriages, abused children, and careers that become jeopardized as these individuals engineer their own destruction, albeit unwittingly.

The executive who is an intensely driven man is more often than not some type of perfectionist—demanding this of himself and others. He requires much affection and approbation. Dr. Margaret Prouty, former chief of pediatrics at Jackson Clinic in Madison, Wisconsin, has reported cyclical occurrences of depression among a selected group of children from seven to nine years old. Her profile of these youngsters corresponds strikingly to the problems of the ambitious, depressive adult. She points to the poor ability they have to express antagonism, and to one of their chief personality defects—an almost total lack of a sense of humor. Life for them is indeed real and earnest and they have no ability to laugh at themselves or others. [5]

This makes the ambitious executive very vulnerable to defeats that move his self-image further away from his ego ideal. A lifetime of such competitive living and being burdened by the threat of failure, explains to a large degree why men resort to suicide. Again, we see the loss of hope and the seeming impossibility of a meaningful future. There is no measure of optimism left and he is overwhelmed by this sense of futility.

ILL HEALTH, DRUGS, ALCOHOL AND SUICIDE

Researchers tell us people who have a low pain threshold are particularly vulnerable to depression. Such persons may be using barbiturates or other prescribed medications. It is no secret that the easy availability of drugs has brought out suicidal tendencies that might otherwise have remained latent.

Myrna Weissman and Karen Fox (Yale University School of Medicine), in their study of 258 men and women admitted to the Yale-New Haven Hospital following unsuccessful suicide attempts, discovered a marked disparity between the seriousness of the intent to commit suicide and the medical complications when an attempt failed. Two-thirds of the group were women. Interviews with the 53 patients who used violent methods (wrist-cutting, shooting, hanging) showed the people who used these methods were more intent on killing themselves than the 205 who took pills. Interestingly enough, when the attempt failed, the medical effects were considerably less for violent attempters. Only 63 percent needed medical attention, compared to 92 percent of the pill poppers. (Pill ingestors also tended to be younger—53 percent were under 26, compared with only 33 percent of those who used knives, ropes and guns.) Researchers point out that what this reveals is an ignorance of the potential lethality of medications in these young attempters. [6]

The sleeplessness brought on by depression will often send a person to the doctor seeking relief. In a moment of desperation, the individual may take all of the sleeping pills.

Ulcers and other physical manifestations of ill health will often force a man, in particular, to think of ending it all. When degenerative diseases set in, there are those who cannot cope with confinement to bed.

If a person has a drinking problem, there is always the potential danger of the combination of drugs with alcohol, a deadly twosome.

INSTALLMENT-PLAN SUICIDES

People who find life intolerable and unmanageable often participate in what psychiatrists call ''death-oriented behavior.'' Alcoholics fit that label. Why does a person drink? Usually, drinking to excess is an attempt to drown one's sorrows; to block out the reality of one's difficult circumstances; to escape responsibility.

Living in a world of isolation, desolation, loneliness, anxiety, fear and uncertainty, such as these have an unconscious desire to end it all. In time they will accomplish what they are unconsciously attempting to do—contributing to their own untimely demise. It is known that alcohol deepens aggressiveness, which, when turned against one's self, may lead directly to a deliberate suicide attempt. Many of these are successful, some because they have gotten behind the wheel of a car.

AUTOCIDE

One of the best places to look for disguised suicides is on the road—traffic fatalities. Has someone ever shot around you on the highway going well beyond the safe driving limits and you say, "Wow, he's going to kill himself!" Precisely. That may be exactly what he is hoping to do. It may be a subconscious wish, but the Federal Center for Studies of Suicide Prevention, Bethseda, Maryland and the Los Angeles Suicide Prevention Center can offer solid evidence that many otherwise inexplicable crashes are actually disguised suicides. Behavioral scientists, as well as police, investigating highway deaths, note such things as dry, straight roads, lack of skid marks, and a car smashed against a tree or a bridge abutment. The report may say "improper driving," but circumstantial evidence strongly supports autocide.

Sociologist David Phillips (University of California, San Diego), did a study paper on his analysis of California traffic fatalities from 1966 to 1973. He compared figures for ordinary weeks with statistics for weeks following suicides that were highly publicized in that state. (Those suicides included playwright William Inge, Japanese novelist Yukio Mishima and California wine maker A. Korbel.) Phillips' findings revealed that on the third day after such a suicide report, auto fatalities rose by 30 percent; then leveled off for the week at 9 percent above normal. "In general," noted Phillips, "the more publicity given to the suicide story, the more the number of auto fatalities rises." [7]

Time magazine (July 11, 1977) reported that except for the Depression year of 1932, the current suicide rate in the United States is the highest in history. In reporting on Phillips' study, they noted that he suggested an exploration into what the psychological and sociological mechanisms are that seem to be operating when someone decides to commit autocide.

SUICIDE BY ARTISTS AND WRITERS

In the three suicides mentioned by Phillips, you will note two of them were writers. Artists and writers by necessity must isolate themselves to do much of their work. They frequently live lonely lives. Isolation is a breeding ground for despair, especially if the "great American novel" isn't so great (*Today's Health,* February, 1976).

I can attest to the loneliness of this type of work. Often it becomes necessary to practically barricade the door, take the phone off the hook, and post a "DO NOT DISTURB" sign. I am frequently accused of being unfriendly and aloof. Few understand the demands creative work imposes upon someone. I spend long, lonely hours at my desk. I have learned to say what I hope amounts to a gracious "No." A good amount of aspiration, inspiration and frustration exists in the life of creative people. Out of all of this, however, emerges writing and artistry in painting and drawing. And it is satisfying. The more disciplined one is, the more that can be accomplished.

Statistics don't show the agony that precipitates the suicide act. Writer Al Alvarez, in telling of his own suicide attempt in the book, *The Savage God: A Study of Suicide*, explains: "Each sporadic burst of work, each minor success and disappointment, each moment of calm and relaxation, seemed merely a temporary halt on my steady descent through layer after layer of depression, like an elevator stopping for a moment on the way down to the basement. At no point was there any question of getting off or changing the direction of the journey." [8] Alvarez attempted suicide by swallowing 45 pills on top of a good deal of alcohol.

The list of gifted creative people who have killed themselves is long. Any such list is tragic. You may recognize some of these names: John Berryman, Anne Sexton, Hart Crane, Virginia Woolf, Sylvia Plath, Ernest Hemingway, Marilyn Monroe, Vincent van Gogh, Thomas Chatterton, and even Socrates.

The San Francisco Golden Gate Bridge has been the jumping off place for many suicides. The first was Harold Wobber, on August 8, 1937, just 73 days after it opened. He died an instant death after hitting the water, 238 feet below. [9] Few survive that leap, but one whose attempt was a "failure," six years later stated: "People become depressed because they have desires and they are not fulfilled. If a person could just realize that those desires are not going to be answered by *wanting* them.'' [10]

How true it is that desire and expectation are potent drives—the very stuff of which life with all its shades of meaning is comprised. Why is it that some are driven to suicidal despair, and others whose desires and expectations are not always met, manage to survive without giving in? Certainly the hopeful balance of expectation and reality keeps most from despair and must be reckoned with. But there are other motivating factors.

WHAT ABOUT SUICIDE AMONG MINORITIES

Success does not always translate into happiness for celebrities. Such was the case for comic Freddie Prinze who used a .32 caliber automatic pistol to put a bullet through his head. The son of a Puerto Rican mother and a Hungarian father, he began looking early in life for a way out of the poverty and petty crime of the neighborhood where his family lived. He was a natural entertainer with a street-wise sense of humor and became a star almost overnight for the "Chico and the Man" series.

Young Prinze couldn't handle the pressures of success and an impending divorce. Veteran comic Jack Albertson, "Chico's" co-star, in commenting on Prinze's suicide (*Newsweek,* February 7, 1977) said, "He was typical of young men who come into fame and fortune at a very early age." Albertson called the whole thing "shocking and sickening," and that suicide definitely is.

What about suicide among minorities: People from all races, creeds, and cultural backgrounds kill themselves. Southern blacks living in rural areas seldom take their lives; but the statistics change drastically in the northern part of the United States. In New York City, the rate of suicides for blacks regularly exceeds the rate for whites. Black people are killing themselves at an increasing rate—especially the men between ages 20 to 40. Forty percent of all black suicides occur in the 20-29 age group.

Ebony magazine (September, 1973) reported that black females are killing themselves at the highest rates recorded in the past 50 years. Among psychiatrists and sociologists specializing in suicide research whose careers have touched the lives of suicidal black people, there is general agreement that anger plays a leading role in suicide among black women.

Dr. Herbert Hendin, a noted New York psychoanalyst who

observed suicidal black people at Harlem Hospital, says: "Among (these) young men and women, I saw great disappointments experienced very early in life. And those disappointments led to an overwhelming sense of rage and frustration, which ultimately led to suicide attempts when the rage and frustration became combined with the sense that nothing was going to change." [11] Black males, according to Dr. Hendin in his book *Black Suicide*, are harder hit by socio-economic pressure; but it is often the female who bears the brunt of his anger.

There are other factors, not necessarily peculiar to blacks and minorities, which show that the number of variables relating to the details of the suicide attempt, such as method, motivation and circumstances preceding the attempt, are not that different (between blacks and whites).

Dr. Ronald W. Maris, professor of sociology at the University of South Carolina and author of *Social Forces in Urban Suicide* states: "Hopelessness and isolation resulting from failed social relationships often lead to suicide. It is not just being alone that causes one to be suicidal. Rather, it is the process of how one came to be alone. What we often see is a whole series of pathological relationships—often starting with a mother and father—which ultimately results in a suicide's negative self-image, low self-esteem and feelings of isolation and rejection. In short, many suicides come from what we call multi-problem families." [12]

Black psychiatrist Dr. James P. Comer, Yale University Medical School and author of *Beyond Black and White*, emphasizes that no single theory or view can explain suicide and that many of the theories embracing black suicide—including his own attempt are speculative. "One of the things we're really talking about is the complexity of suicide, the complexity of the suicidal process . . . suicide among black people is rendered even more complex by the present changes taking place in black culture." Those changes include the decline of the church and the destruction of "the closely knit communities in which one had a sense of belonging. In fact, suicide rates are going up for everybody—white and black, men and women—because urban living produces the opportunity not to feel a part of things." [13]

Among Blacks, Chicanos and American Indians, the suicide rate drops after age 44. This contrasts with the pattern among whites, where, according to psychologist Richard Seiden, the risk of suicide rises with increasing age. [14]

STATUS-INTEGRATION

Dr. Seiden believes that when things get better for minorities, they can also get worse, i.e., poverty among blacks conferred some sort of immunity to suicide because many blacks had low aspirations. Now blacks can worry about reaching their potentials, economically and socially, and when that doesn't happen, it's much more devastating.

This sheds some light on the rise in black suicides—as more blacks have become middle class in recent years, the suicide rate has increased.

POPULATION SHIFTS

When minorities move from rural to urban areas, and from South to North, there is a resulting breakdown of families, unemployment, cramped tenements and other factors which contribute to rage and frustration. It is pointed out that many black suicides, unlike white suicides, are an outgrowth of difficulties with authorities and police. Much of this can be traced to problems that arise with geographic mobility and high unemployment among adult black males.

Still another theory advanced which shows a similarity between blacks and whites committing suicide may be the importance of the loss of a father figure. Dr. Seiden points to a study of white men who graduated from Ivy League colleges in the 1920s and killed themselves thirty years later. The study showed father-figure loss to be one of the most important factors.

Studies of the Indian population in this country have uncovered a virtual suicide epidemic among Indian adolescents between fifteen and twenty years of age. The attempt rate, however, among Navajo Indians in the United States was not found to be high. Indians with nontraditional backgrounds were among the attempters. The characteristics of Navajo attempters were similar to attempters from other groups.[15] The problem Indian adolescents face, relates to identity. He is caught between two cultures; he is neither an Indian, with a sense of pride and respect for his people and his culture, nor an assimilated outsider able to identify with the culture and traditions of the dominant group. The result is psychologic chaos.[16]

THE SINGLE GENERAL COMMON DENOMINATOR

Dr. Norman Farberow was asked by the Los Angeles *Times Home* Magazine (June 2, 1974) if there was a single common denominator as cause (in most suicides). ''Most often we find it's a threat of or actual rupture of a relationship,'' he replied. ''A person is upset at being rejected and at having to face the future alone. Usually it comes down to whether a person feels alone, unloved, inadequate.''

Someone has said that as children we outgrew our fear of the dark by opening our eyes to the night. As adults we must take a larger step toward maturity by opening our eyes to our mortality and to the understanding that within our bodies are planted the seeds of both life and death. In the Book of Ecclesiastes we are told that there is a time to be born and a time to die. Actually we die a little daily for within our bodies are planted by the Creator Himself, the seeds of both life and death. But to hasten that death through suicide is, as Immanuel Kant wrote, an insult to humanity.

Death is a robber. That fact cannot be denied. But death by suicide brings the greatest affront to all who remain. What is the answer to living and dying? Is it *people?* Position? Things? Is it a recovery of hope? Hope in what? Hope in who? If hope moves a person out of suicidal preoccupation, then in what should one hope? We recognize that hope must be based on reality factors. The writer of Psalms provides the answer—an answer we shall explore in more detail. David cried out in his distress:

> I am benumbed and badly crushed;
> I groan because of the agitation of my heart.
> Lord, all my desire is before Thee;
> And my sighing is not hidden from Thee.
> My heart throbs, my strength fails me . . .
> My loved ones and my friends stand aloof . . .
> And my kinsmen stand afar off . . .
> [But] I hope in Thee, O Lord:
> Thou wilt answer, O Lord my God . . .
> For I am ready to fall . . .
> Lord, make me to know my end,
> And what is the extent of my days,
> Let me know how transient I am.

Behold, Thou hast made my days as handbreadths,
And my lifetime as nothing in Thy sight,
Surely every man at his best is a mere breath . . .
And now, Lord, for what do I wait?
My hope is in Thee.

(Selected portions from Psalm 38:8-11, 15, 17
and 39:4-5, 7 *NASB*)

1. Marshall Berges, ''The Norman Farberows,'' Los Angeles *Times Home* magazine (June 2, 1974), p. 45.

2. Michael P. Scott, ''Suicide: Let's Separate Fact From Fiction,'' *Better Homes and Gardens* (April, 1977).

3. Earl A. Grollman, *Suicide* (Boston: Beacon Press, 1971), p. 56.

4. Ibid.

5. Harry Levinson, ''On Executive Suicide,'' *Harvard Business Review* (July, 1975), pp. 120, 121.

6. ''Drugs and Suicide— A Problem On Both Sides of the Atlantic,'' *Psychology Today* (September, 1973), p. 6.

7. ''Suicide by Auto,'' *Time* (July 11, 1977), p. 62.

8. Al Alvarez, *The Savage God: A Study of Suicide* (New York: Random House, Inc., 1972).

9. ''Esthetics of Suicide,'' *Newsweek* (January 9, 1961), p. 25.

10. Nora Gallagher, ''Why People Kill Themselves,'' *Today's Health* (February, 1976), p. 50.

11. ''Suicide, A Growing Menace,'' *Ebony* (September, 1973).

12. Ibid.

13. Ibid.

14. ''The Misunderstood Matter of Suicide, '' *Psychology Today,* (December, 1974), p. 138.

15. Myrna M. Weissman, ''The Epidemiology of Suicide Attempts, 1960 to 1971,'' New Haven, Conn., *Arch. Gen. Psychiatry/*Vol. 30 (June, 1974), p. 744.

16. Earl A. Grollman, *Suicide* (Boston: Beacon Press, 1971), p. 61.

7

Suicide is a fatal game that leads from
lucidity in the face of existence to
a flight from light.
Albert Camus

By Any Name,
It's Tragic

Those who die for their faith, their strong beliefs, or for a cause we call martyrs.

Those who die in the line of duty, such as servicemen, we call heroes.

Those who die saving others we call brave and selfless.

And those who die by their own hand we call suicides.

Death before dishonor and suicide for love have been popular themes among poets and playwrights for centuries. On paper or on the stage, the suffering of a tragic hero or heroine who ends up taking his or her own life is often made to appear somewhat noble. But in actual life there is nothing grandiose about the act at all. It has been said that suicide is ugly for onlookers, devastating for relatives, and harrowing even for those professionally involved. Anyone who has been at all close to a suicidal situation knows it is impossible to come away remaining aloof and unfeeling.

COPPING OUT RATHER THAN COPING

Suicide frequency increases with age. This is a sad commentary. Goals have not been attained. Hopes lie unrealized. Marital and family conflicts exist. The middle-aged person who takes a serious look at his life and does not like what he sees in the past and what looms ahead for the future decides that copping out is better than coping. Failure, defeat, tiredness—who needs more of that? It's called the midlife crisis. Aspiration becomes frustration, and suicide is often the end result.

THE FORGOTTEN ELDERLY

Then there are the forgotten elderly. Annually they top the statistics of those whose suicide has been completed. How dreadfully sad and revealing. The evening paper carries the distressing news that an elderly California man shoots and kills his wife in their home and then, turning the .45-caliber automatic on himself commits suicide. This would be called a murder-suicide pact, not at all an uncommon occurrence among suicide statistics among the elderly.

The religious community was shocked in March, 1975 when the New York *Times* revealed that one of the world's preeminent Presbyterians, the Reverend Henry Pitney Van Dusen, 77, and his wife Elizabeth, 80, had carried out a suicide pact in January. The retired president of New York's Union Theological Seminary and Mrs. Van Dusen took overdoses of sleeping pills in their Princeton, New Jersey home. It was reported that she died quickly, but he vomited up the pills, was found and taken to a hospital, where he died a month later of a heart attack (*Times* magazine, March 10, 1975).

The California couple mentioned first, left a note citing failing health as the reason. The Van Dusen's left behind a note also declaring that theirs was a responsible decision that "will become more usual and acceptable as the years pass." Van Dusen was known as a nonstop churchman, heading Union at its pinnacle of influence. In 1970 he suffered a stroke. This forced him into retirement. It was reported that he had little pain and could walk with a cane, but his speech was largely incomprehensible. That, of course, was a severe frustration for a man with his verbal skill. Mrs. Van Dusen suffered from arthritis and had undergone two hip surgeries. Their suicide pact was not made under the extreme conditions of terminal illness that is often seen in such situations. Their note stated, "We are both increasingly weak and unwell, and who would want to die in a nursing home?" [1]

GOOD DEATH?

Van Dusen was an adviser of the Euthanasia Council. The word *euthanasia* means literally "good death." In 1967 he proposed that the time might come when persons could decide to have their lives ended in cases of "total mental and spiritual disability." He supported, however, only the right to die without being kept alive by heroic support measures. That is called "passive" euthanasia and differs from "active" euthanasia, or "mercy killing."

There was divergence of opinion among Van Dusen friends, whom *Time* magazine called "a *Who's Who* of liberal Protestantism." The magazine reported that his colleagues were, for the most part, sympathetic.

OR BONHOEFFER'S VIEW?

Holding a different view, however, was Dietrich Bonhoeffer. His death was the result of being executed by the Nazis. (Bonhoeffer, interestingly, was an illustrious Union Theological Seminary alumnus.) Bonhoeffer was in opposition to suicide and stated: "God has reserved to Himself the right to determine the end of life, because He alone knows the goal to which it is His will to lead it. Even if (a person's) earthly life has become a torment for him, he must commit it intact to God's hands, from which it came." Bonhoeffer was expressing what has always been one of the bedrock "thou-shalt-nots" of Judeo-Christendom.

THE HUMANIST'S VIEW

Throughout history there have been those logicians—from Socrates to Bertrand Russell—who have branded this biblical concept as irrational, antilibertarian and unenforceable. And logicians do not give up. In their "rational broadsides" and "humanistic manifestos" signed by intellectual grandees they assert the absolute right of the individual to control his or her own bodily destiny in regard to reproduction, medical treatment or lack of it, and termination, including euthanasia and suicide. We shall be hearing much more of this in the times in which we are living. In recent years abortion, women's liberation and "gay liberation" have dominated the news. Manifesto mongering has made an impact.

Dr. Thomas Szasz, whom *Newsweek* magazine labeled "a radical psychiatrist ("The Myth of Mental Illness") and "strong humanist sympathizer," states: "Jewish fundamentalism said God owns everything, and Christianity picked up this idea and elaborated it. But since the seventeenth century, with the rise of science, doctors have been saying, 'Take the power over the body away from God and give it to me.' So, who has ownership—the person himself or the doctors?" [2]

Christians would be quick to point to such places in the Bible as 1 Corinthians 6:19,20 and give answer to that line of questioning. "Your own body does not belong to you. For God has bought you with a great price. So use every part of your body to give glory back to God, because he owns it."

Throughout the Bible that teaching is underscored—we do not belong to ourselves. "Behold, all souls are mine" (Ezekiel 18:4, *KJV*). "The Lord kills, The Lord gives life" (1 Samuel 2:6). It would appear that God is saying that when He gives us life, we are not to say yes to death by our own volition and will; He reserves to Himself the right of life *and* death.

Always the Bible shows the value of life and makes statements giving life principles. God is the giver and sustainer of life for anyone and everyone. There are those, however, who refuse to acknowledge the sovereignty of God. There are those also who question why a loving God allows suffering. Even though life may appear to be a series of empty endless tomorrows, we, as the apostle Paul has written, do not know enough to be God's counselor and guide. We are not calling the plays, much as we'd like to think we are; God is in control. He holds the reins of life *and* death.

"CALLERS DON'T JUMP; JUMPERS DON'T CALL!"

Humanists question the assumption that modern medicine's knowledge of the dynamics of suicide is any more scientific than the East African witch doctor's curse or the "old Christian idea of diabolic possession" (*Newsweek*, October 29, 1973). For some years there has been strong debate about the effectiveness of suicide-prevention centers with sociologists like Dr. Donald Light Jr., Princeton University, taking the opposing view. "Most people who call in are are not suicidal," and most individuals contemplating suicide do not call in." They point to statistics and studies which show no significant decreases in suicide rates where such suicide prevention centers exist. But those involved with such centers would be equally quick to point to results they have documented. As *Newsweek* states: "No compilation of statistics is likely to stunt the determination of doctors and social workers to try to reach suicidal persons—with or without success."

Many social scientists will argue the right of the individual to terminate his life. Elizabeth Herzog White had a long and successful career as a social scientist. But in August, 1972, she wrote a brief note to her "nears-and-dears" that began with the startling words, "I am committing euthanasia."

What brought her to that decision? She was 71 and suffering from cancer that was spreading and incurable. Her husband explained, "She was very eager to protect me from any charge of collusion in her suicide. She went to a hotel room, leaving me another note saying, 'Don't try to find me, you can't. I've left the area.' " The next day she was found dead of an overdose of seconal in a downtown Washington hotel. Her husband is convinced that deliberate suicide like this to escape months of pointless suffering is justified.

The same newspaper that carried the story of Elizabeth Herzog White told of Dr. Garnett Bale, a family doctor practicing in Elizabethport, Kentucky who diagnosed a tumor of the brain in himself. Methodist Hospital in Louisville confirmed his diagnosis and the prognosis was bad: death in three to six months. He returned to his own hospital, Hardin County Memorial, to be near home. His wife explained: "Aware that paralysis, blindness and complete loss of controls would accompany those few months, he quietly began to refuse all foods and fluids. Assuring him that we respected his wishes, we asked him to let us know quickly if he should change his mind. He never did. He lasted twelve days." [3]

A GROWING TIDE OF SENTIMENT

In the cases of both Dr. Bale and Betty Herzog White, there was much understanding from friends and colleagues. It would appear that there is a growing tide of sentiment that says under such circumstances suicide should be accepted in Western society.

Dr. Szasz (professor of psychiatry at State University of New York at Syracuse), says "suicide should be discouraged, but in the end the patient has a right to take his life." [4]

VIEWS OF THE CLERGY

Reverend Warren Briggs, a Methodist minister, agrees with the views espoused by the humanists and he is not alone. "When circumstances become such that one's physical life has no meaning, no dignity, no value to the individual or society, the individual should have the right to choose when and how he is to escape the indignity, the pain the futility of physical existence." [5]

It is safe to say, however, that most theologians would hold to the view of Bonhoeffer (expressed earlier in this chapter).

What we have to realize here is that suicide in terminal illness and self-destruction in the full vigor of life are two different things. Even those with the humanist view would not condone suicide among the very young.

Those clergymen who espouse "passive euthanasia" or the right to die in terminal illness without extraordinary means being used to prolong life, are those who have witnessed the pain and suffering of the terminally ill. Reverend Robert B. Reeves, Jr., chaplain of Presbyterian Hospital in New York and a faculty member at Columbia University states: "We have somehow got to a vitalistic tack that has made simple biological continuance the absolute good. And it seems to me that this is a perversion of the Judeo-Christian value scheme. The supreme value in our religious heritage is placed on the personhood of man, the person in his wholeness, the person in his freedom, the person in his integrity and dignity.

"When illness brings a person to a state in which he is less than a free person, less than one with integrity and dignity, then what is most valuable and precious is gone, and we may well feel that his mere continuance by machine or drugs is a violation of him as a person." [6]

Edward J. Doherty (North American Newspaper Alliance) in reporting on the morality of the issue stated that Jews appear to be lagging behind Christians in supporting "passive euthanasia," and that the Pope speaking for the Roman Catholics seems to support the principle of "passive euthanasia." [7]

The New York office of the Euthanasia Educational Council has sent out many hundreds of thousands of copies of the "Living Will." It is something the living can fill out and sign before witnesses and dispatch to their next-of-kin, their doctor, lawyer or clergyman. It is not legally binding, but it enables an individual while he is mentally competent and in good health to make known his wishes to others as to how he feels about prolonging terminal illness. Needless to say, this has caused considerable anguish in the medical profession. [8]

Dr. Elizabeth Kubler-Ross, the Chicago psychiatrist who has made a study of death and dying by interviewing more than five hundred patients with terminal illnesses, and who has written the best-seller *On Death and Dying* has stated: "Our basic role should be to relieve suffering and not to prolong life. I am against any form or shape of mercy killings; I want to make this very clear. But I am very, very much in favor of allowing patients to die with dignity; the patient's own death.

"I am very opposed to artificial prolongation of life when it becomes meaningless . . . [9]

LESSONS FROM HISTORY

The apostle Paul, in his writings, speaks of our bodies as being "perishable containers" and "weak" (2 Corinthians 4:7). There is an interesting story in the New Testament book of Acts in which we see Paul and his companion Silas imprisoned in Philippi. Roman custom dictated that the prison jailer was responsible for the prisoners. While Paul and Silas were in jail there was a great earthquake about midnight. "The foundations of the prison-house were shaken; and immediately all the doors were opened, and everyone's chains were unfastened" (Acts 16:26 NASB).

Startled from his sleep, the jailer looked about in total dismay. The cell doors were all open. The prisoners, he presumed, had all fled. His reaction was characteristic of a Roman soldier—he would rather kill himself than to incur the disgrace of failure. In a moment of panic, "he drew his sword and was about to kill himself . . ." (v. 27).

What does the Bible have to say to a person who is in the midst of an earthquake experience. The Christian world points to this and similar biblical accounts to stress that God is not an absentee omnipotent who can't be bothered with the cries of despairing people. To the panic-stricken heart, regardless of their "earthquake-type" experience, the answer to the question, "What must I do?" is the same. It's a hopeful answer, "Do yourself no harm" (v. 28). Paul was in effect shouting to the jailer, "Suicide is *not* the way out of your plight."

A close look at the New Testament, however, shows only indirect reference to suicide. Although the Apostle's writings are liberally sprinkled with exhortations never to give up, the word "suicide" itself and the act are *not* mentioned.

But the teaching that God-given life is a mystery and a beautiful gift is prominent. At the very outset of creation, the Bible records that "God saw everything that He had made, and behold it was very good'' (Genises 1:31a, *KJV*). Other translations and paraphrases say ''it was fitting, pleasant, excellent—and God approved of what had been made completely.'' This is a theses that has stood the test of time. *Life is good.* It is to be emphasized that we are not to despair of its possibilities even though today may look very black. Situations change. People change. Paul said:

''These troubles and sufferings are, after all, quite small and won't last very long. Yet this short time of distress will result in God's richest blessing upon us forever and ever! So we do not look at what we can see right now, the troubles all around us, but we look forward to the joys in heaven which we have not yet seen. The troubles will soon be over, but the joys to come will last forever'' (2 Corinthians 4:17-18).

THE HERETICS AND AUGUSTINE'S INFLUENCE

Alvarez and others have concluded that Christian teaching was at first a powerful incitement to suicide in that the more powerfully the Church instilled in believers the idea that this world was a vale of tears filled with sin and temptation, the more irresistible the temptation to suicide or martyrdom became. The teachings of many of the early church fathers became so extreme, however, that the Church eventually declared them heretics. It was Augustine (A.D. 354-430) who first denounced suicide as a sin. He asserted that ''suicide is an act which precludes the possibility of repentance, and it is a form of homicide and thus a violation of the Decalogue Article, 'Thou shalt not kill.' ''

Augustine's reference is, of course, to the sixth of the Ten Commandments. He taught that the individual who killed himself broke this commandment and became a murderer. That is a sin. A man can be saved by seeking God's forgiveness from sin and claiming the finished work of Christ on the Cross, but how can a dead man repent? Thus Augustine argued. And since life is the gift of God, everything that happens to us, even our sufferings, is divinely ordained and not to be shortened by one's own actions. We are to bear patiently whatever God wills for our lives. To take one's life, Augustine maintained, was not to accept divine will.

We must reckon with the fact that Augustine was a powerful early Church figure, and his arguments were listened to with respect. Largely because of him the door for escape from this life—suicide—was slammed shut. ''The decent alternative of the

Romans, the key to Paradise of the early Christians, had become the most deadly of mortal sins.''[10]

SAINT BRUNO

In the eleventh century, another towering Church figure, Saint Bruno, was to come along and call suicide ''martyrs for Satan,'' which left no room for doubt about what he and others like him thought of the act.

SAINT THOMAS AQUINAS

Two centuries later, Saint Thomas Aquinas, another strong voice in Church history, opposed suicide on the basis of three powerful postulates: (1) It was against the natural inclinations of preservation of life and charity toward the self; (2) It was a trespass against the community; and (3) It was a trespass against God, who had given man life.

In the long superstitious centuries between Augustine and Aquinas, suicide became the most mortal of Christian sins. Many self-murders were denied funeral rites and respectful burial in what was considered holy ground.

THE SEVENTEENTH CENTURY

In the seventeenth century, new philosophical currents of thought began to sweep through the Christian Church. John Donne, it is believed, was one of the first to start a chain reaction against the prevailing attitudes of the Church toward suicide. Suicide, up until then, had been labeled as unclean, damned, and degraded. Donne wrote the first English defense of suicide, *Biathanatos. A Declaration of that Paradoxe, or Thesis, That Self-homicide is not so naturally Sinne, that it may never be otherwise.*

Donne wrote about suicide because he himself was tempted to it. He was a masterful writer, but this book was considered one of his less appealing writings. Later when he became the most famous preacher of his day, it was to become a source of embarrassment to him. Written in the context of depression, Alvarez wonders if it didn't begin as a prelude to self-destruction and actually finish as a substitute for it. ''That is, he set out to find precedents and reasons for killing himself while still remaining Christian—or, at least, without damning himself eternally. But the process of writing the book and marshaling his intricate learning and dialectical skill may have relieved the tension and helped to reestablish his sense of his self."[11] And one might add, his sense of God and divine will.

In the case of John Donne, his Christian training and devotion, like his intellectual energy, were ultimately stronger than his despair. Donne finally negotiated his middle-life crisis by taking holy orders instead of his life. Donne, like others before and after him, heeded the apostle Paul's cry, "Don't give up and quit!"

BUT WHAT ABOUT THE ELDERLY?

As I write this, I am not unaware of the financial burdens, the insecurity, terrible loneliness, defects in vision and hearing, and degenerative diseases that make living unbearable and contribute to the desire to self-destruct. The forgotten and lonely elderly, feeling useless, unneeded, and a burden to their family or society, choose suicide—yes, death seems better than four walls, no companionship, and the inevitable suffering that accompanies ill health in old age.

Did David, the psalmist, looking down the corridor of the years and seeing what lay ahead for himself in old age, feel prompted to write: "Cast me not off in the time of old age; forsake me not when my strength faileth" (Psalm 71:9, KJV)

Did David, facing feelings of hopelessness and despair, cry out in his soul's distress, "I am standing here depressed and gloomy . . . all your waves and billows have gone over me, and floods of sorrow pour upon me like a thundering cataract" (Psalm 42:6a, 7). Did he contemplate suicide? We do not know. We do know, however, that David had great cause for seeking escape, yet he came to his senses time after time. He laid hold upon God's help and cried out,

> "But I will meditate upon your kindness . . . Day by day the Lord pours out his steadfast love upon me, and through the night I sing his songs and pray to God who gives me life.
>
> ". . . O my soul, don't be discouraged! Don't be upset! Expect God to act. For I know that I shall again have plenty of reason to praise him for all that he will do! He is my help! He is my God!" (Psalm 42:11 and elsewhere).

David recognized that human life is of value to God even when downcast.

SECOND THOUGHTS ABOUT DEATH

David summed up his second thoughts about death and his problems very well when he said, "For if I die I cannot give you glory by praising you before my friends (Psalm 6:5).

David had learned what all of us need to understand. We are not promised immunity from periods of despondency, sickness, financial reverses, or problems of one kind or another regardless of our age. But God does exist. He is always there to comfort and to make us strong even in our moments of greatest weakness. How does one escape from the kind of despair that drives one to the very brink of suicide? Moses, Elijah, Paul, David, and a host of others before us have discovered that it is always safe to flee to God. And it is *not* a sign of mistrust in God to seek out the help of others highly competent who stand ready with professional know-how.

1. "Good Death?" *Time* (March 10, 1975), p. 83.

2. "Now, A Right to Suicide," *Newsweek* (October 29, 1973), p. 78.

3. "The Right To Die," "Is Suicide Ever Acceptable," Fullerton, Ca., *Daily News Tribune* (March 1, 1973), p. A-7.

4. Ibid.

5. Ibid.

6. "The Right To Die,", "The Morality of The Issue," Fullerton, Ca., *Daily News Tribune* (March 3, 1973), p. A-7.

7. Ibid.

8. Ibid.

9. Ibid., "Man on Spot—The Doctor" (March 4, 1973).

10. Al Alvarez, *The Savage God: A Study of Suicide* (New York: Random House, 1972).

11. Ibid.

> Every suicide has an unsolvable and
> unsharable problem in the mind.
> Emile Durkheim

Suicide: The Abyss of Dark Pessimism

At one time it was believed that almost all suicides were victims of insanity. There are still those who will insist that if not total insanity, then temporary insanity propels a person to take his own life. But most studies and most psychologists, psychiatrists, and others who work in the field of suicidology will tell you that the great majority of suicides are in touch with reality; they may be desperate, it is true, but they are normal people.

Psychological studies reveal that before the desperate act of self-execution, 80 percent of suicide victims had consulted their family physician, 17 percent had visited a psychiatrist, 7 percent had sought help from a social agency, and 2 percent had taken counsel with either a rabbi, a minister, or a priest.

Not only is it important for the physician, nurse, social worker, and clergyman to be aware of and recognize what may amount to suicidal threats, but each of us also has a responsibility to members of our family and friends to keep the lines of communication open and to demonstrate love. For too long, society has simply condemned suicide. With society becoming more complex, with more people despairing, we need to understand what it is that drives a person to self-murder, and we must take steps to prevent it.

SUICIDE PREVENTION CENTERS

Many communities have established suicide prevention centers; most of the major cities throughout the country have around-the-clock lifelines for potential suicides. Such telephone numbers are advertised in local papers and news sheets where area suicide prevention centers are located. A directory of some of these centers can be found in the Appendix of this book.

SUICIDERS ANONYMOUS

Many churches have stepped into the act, maintaining "Help-line" telephone counseling. Caring individuals in such church and community centers are doing much to sustain life. Coinciding with publication of this book is the launching of *Suiciders Anonymous* nationwide from the Garden Grove Community Church, Garden Grove, California (known for its television program "Hour of Power" and the dynamic ministry of its pastor, Dr. Robert Schuller). *Suiciders Anonymous* is a self-help group, patterned after *Alcoholics Anonymous* with groups meeting in Southern California areas at the time of this writing. As explained in their literature the sole requirement for membership is a sincere desire to recover from the depths that led to a suicide attempt. It is open to those professionals and lay persons also who are interested in the recovery process.

Suiciders Anonymous has a 12-step program:

(1) I admit that on my own I cannot make my life turn out right.

(2) I believe that only with the help of a Power greater than myself can I recover harmony and hope in my life.

(3) I decide to turn my will, my life and all I have over to the care of God, as I have come to understand Him.

(4) I am making a searching and fearless inventory of myself— my shortcomings and my strengths.

(5) I admit to God, to myself, and to another human being the exact nature of both my shortcomings and strengths.

(6) I am ready to have God remove my shortcomings and improve my strengths.

(7) With God's help, I correct my shortcomings and build on my strengths.

(8) I make a list of all individuals whom I have wronged, and become willing to make amends to them all.

(9) I make direct amends to such people, whenever possible, except when to do so would injure them or others.

(10) I continue to take personal inventory. When I am wrong, I promptly admit it; when I am strong, I promptly celebrate it.

(11) I seek through study, meditation, and two-way prayer to improve my conscious awareness of God, as I understand Him, seeking knowledge of His will for me and the strength to carry it out.

(12) Having had a spiritual awakening, as a result of these 12 steps, I seek to practice these principles and seek to relate them to others who also are seeking solutions to their problems and new hope for their lives.

For further information write *Suiciders Anonymous*, Garden Grove Community Church, Garden Grove, California 92640.

CONTACT TELEMINISTRIES

Another organization with a history dating back to 1966 and a work begun in Sydney, Australia, as *Life Line*, by Dr. Alan Walker at the Central Methodist Mission, is the CONTACT Teleministry Movement. Centers in the United States are affiliated with an international secretariat sponsoring teleministry centers in Australia, Canada, Japan, Korea, New Zealand, South Africa and Taiwan.

Local CONTACT centers are now operating in cities throughout the United States. These ecumenical ministries reach out in the name of Christ to make help as close as the telephone. Specifically Christian in approach, according to Executive Director Robert E. Larson, these centers offer "a place to turn when in despair," with accredited workers trained to handle a variety of crises, including suicide.

Literature published by CONTACT Teleministries explains that there are many ways to call for help, but by far the most easily available means is the telephone. The telephone is not only a means of emergency assistance, it is also an instrument of human compassion and a lifeline of hope. For the millions of Americans in the areas served by CONTACT, there is an instantaneous, omnipresent source of help. When they are called they are assured of being immediately in touch with a person who cares and is prepared to listen, to understand, and trained to offer help.

Director Larson emphasizes that there's a difference between crisis intervention and crisis interference. A crisis is never static. It usually develops over a period of time and reaches a critical moment. What happens then can have a profound influence on the resolution of the crisis and on the future life history of the persons involved.

Larson explains that effective intervention in these critical situations depends very much on the moment. It can be interfered with too soon or too late. It can be seen, therefore, that the effectiveness of a crisis intervention ministry depends on its availability at the right moment and on the competency of the helping agent.

The CONTACT model is built around well-motivated, highly trained volunteers who are prepared and ready to put themselves ''on the line,'' to become involved with another person at the point of his pain, and to extend the healing resources of the Gospel with a helping hand. Listening ears *and* helping hands make CONTACT a realistic, purposeful, and redemptive model for ministry.

Larson says, ''This expertise is the measure of CONTACT's success as a crisis intervention ministry. We need to continue guarding against the often expressed attitude that one doesn't have to think or know anything—just feel and act kindly—in order to help another person. We can hardly spend too much time learning and developing the necessary skills of effective crisis intervention.''

Look magazine (August 23, 1966) called these telephone life-lines ''strands of hope in a tragic situation.'' By persuading these desperate callers to wait, they can be saved and helped. The conversations that take place are matters of life and death.

The reader is well-advised to get in touch with CONTACT Teleministries if your church recognizes the need and is prepared to develop a 24-hour-a-day telephone ''hotline'' crisis-intervention center. In many cities local ministeriums and councils of churches as well as mental health associations work together in providing this service for a given area.

A GRIMLY DEPERSONALIZED WORLD

No one will deny that we are living in a grimly depersonalized world. These Helpline numbers make it possible, despite the grim depersonalization imposed in our overgrown cities, for would-be suicides to cut through bureaucratic apathy and red tape to get the help they need so desperately. Much of the time all they need is someone to talk to. They live in a world surrounded by people, but no one says ''hello,'' or inquires about their needs.

A nurse in the emergency room in Chicago's giant Cook County Hospital says: "We often see the same patients again and again. Their wrists bear old scars, from two or three previous attempts." Yes, these surely are people crying out for help, but too often, cries go unheard.

Dr. Thaddeus Kostrubala (formerly Chicago's mental-health director) has been quoted as stating that the public attitude toward suicide is weak, sinful and a disgrace. [1]

In many cities, up to 90 percent of the suicidal patients are discharged without further treatment after their stomachs are pumped or their wrists sewn up. "We send ten percent of them—the worst risks—to a state hospital so they won't be able to harm themselves," says Dr. Vladimir Urse, superintendent of Cook County Hospital's mental-health clinic. [2] Outpatient clinics and care facilities cost money. Generally these desperate people do not have that kind of money, and besides, it takes months to get into such places. The reader can plainly see the immensity of the problems posed by suicide in the nation.

Dr. Philip Solomon, associate professor of psychiatry at Harvard Medical School, who has done a great deal to prevent suicides, believes that psychiatrists and treatment facilities alone cannot do the job. "There will never be enough psychiatrists for this—not even physicians, nurses and ministers. [3]

RESCUE, INC.

In Boston, Dr. Solomon has been working with *Rescue, Inc.*, a nondenominational suicide-prevention group which was originally organized by a Catholic priest, Father Kenneth B. Murphy, whom police frequently summoned to talk would-be suicides out of leaping to their deaths.

The calls received by *Rescue, Inc.*, are typical of such calls received in similar rescue centers, and come not only from would-be suicides, but from people trapped in such problems as sickness, poverty and loneliness, anyone of which can precipitate a suicide crisis.

THE LOS ANGELES SUICIDE PREVENTION CENTER

Perhaps the best known rescue organization is the Los Angeles Suicide Prevention Center. Begun in 1958, it keeps its phone lines open around the clock. This emergency facility has spawned helplines and crises centers across the nation with mental health professionals, and a corps of volunteers who fight fiercely to save lives. The days at such centers are tension-packed with everyone working feverishly to help the lonely people who speak haunting messages of desperation.

The founders of the Los Angeles center are two clinical psychologists, Dr. Edwin S. Shneidman and Dr. Norman L. Farberow. The experiences of these Los Angeles researchers have proved invaluable to the National Institute of Mental Health which wages a constant battle in the war against suicide.

BASICALLY, WHAT DO SUCH CENTERS PROVIDE?

Basically, the center provides three kinds of activities:

Clinical—it seeks, through crisis intervention to stop people from killing themselves.

Research—it seeks to understand why people take their own lives.

Training—it seeks to teach others how to deal with suicidal behavior.

In the Los Angeles *Times Home* magazine interview (June 2, 1974) Dr. Farberow explained the procedure in handling calls. All callers are dealt with in a gentle, kindly way and are put through an interview. "The objective is to establish rapport," he explained "so the person doesn't feel alone. We let the caller know that we're interested, concerned, expert, and that we can help. We communicate this quickly by the questions we ask."

The primary task is to help the person survive through this immediate time of crisis. By getting the individual to talk, the phone counselors get into the details of the event that kicked off the crisis, and are better able to convey the impression that they understand what's been happening in the depths of the caller's misery.

Because of the tremendous number of calls received, plus the repeat calls, the center is not able to tell every caller to come in for help. "Our approach from the outset was to develop a way of treatment on the telephone," Dr. Farberow explains.

FOCUS

About 60 percent of the callers are the suicidal persons themselves, the other 40 percent being divided among family and friends of the suicidal persons, professional sources and others. 12 percent of the suicidal persons are considered ''seriously suicidal.''

''A suicidal person is completely chaotic, disorganized, confused, with all kinds of problems weighing in at once. This means that it isn't necessary for us to choose *the* problem that's most pressing. If we can pick out *one* problem, it helps the person to focus and to begin work on something that's feasible to resolve.'' So an important part of the telephone work is to help the caller *focus*.

When the caller has already begun the suicide act, it is the center's job to get medical help to the individual right away. At other times the caller may have pills or a gun at hand. You can quickly see the importance of the telephone counselor's role. The caller also looks for outside resources near at hand to come to the help of the caller—acquaintances, family, friends, co-workers. This information must be extracted from the caller.

A DISPOSITION PLAN

Farberow explained that the counselor must always have a disposition plan, i.e., he must determine while talking to the individual what is the best plan of action. If the caller is concerned, for instance, that he has cancer, the telephone counselor will say, ''I'm going to help you by making an appointment for you at a clinic nearby. I'd like you to go there tomorrow.''

The reasoning back of this tact is that ''By giving the person something to do, a definite *assignment*, he suddenly has a specific point in the future on which to hang his hat.'' [4]

The efforts of the volunteer worker can be distilled into six facets whereby he or she seeks: (1) To establish a relationship with the caller; (2) To clarify the problems; (3) To evaluate the caller's suicide potential; (4) To assess his strengths and resources; (5) To formulate a plan of therapy; and (6) To mobilize the resources.

CHRONIC TROUBLE CALLERS

Many centers receive calls from people who are in chronic trouble. Their problems are long-term situations. The Los Angeles Center deals with them through group therapy programs, but these are not among the suicidal individuals. Self-destruction is only one point in the spectrum of self-injurious behavior. Many cities have drug rehabilitation centers running in conjunction with the efforts of the Suicide Prevention Center.

THE LANGUAGE OF CRISIS

"Suicidal people are *made,* not born," stresses Dr. Farberow. In order to *unmake* them, suicidal behaviorists and "gatekeepers" must learn more about the roots of self-destructive behavior and the various forms which these beginnings foster. "The language of crisis is filled with unexpected twists and turns," he states.

WHO ARE THE "GATEKEEPERS"?

"Gatekeepers" is possibly a new term to the average reader. Farberow uses that term to refer to a person who is not a professional in the field of mental health but who is likely to meet people who are suicidal. "These would be police, clergymen, lawyers or teachers. A large part of our effort is aimed at these groups. The goal is to educate them to not draw back in horror if someone professes to be suicidal. The gatekeepers can help by being *concerned* and by *trying* to help." [5]

1. Jack Star, "Suicide, A New Attack Against An Old Killer, *Look*, (August 23, 1966), p. 60.
2. Ibid.
3. Ibid.
4. "The Norman Farberows," by Marshall Berges, Los Angeles *Times Home* magazine (June 2, 1974), p. 46.
5. Ibid, pp. 46, 51.

> Have courage for the great sorrows of life,
> and patience for the small ones, and
> when you have laboriously accomplished
> your daily task, go to sleep in peace.
> God is awake.
> Victor Hugo

9

The Needless Killer

Consider these cries:

"Lord, take away my life . . ."

or

"O Lord, take my life from me, for it is better for me to die than to live . . ."

or

"I am not able to bear all this . . . It is too heavy for me . . . Kill me, I pray thee."

Sound familiar? Perhaps you've anguished in prayer like that or someone you know has cried out like this. They may have even ended up a suicide statistic.

MOSES

Are you aware that those cries were uttered by some very well-known Bible characters? Moses—remember him? He had achieved stupendous things for God and his nation, but he carried some unbelievable burdens on his shoulders. It was he who, physically exhausted, overtaxed by the unremitting daily strain of maintaining liaison between God and a nation of two million discontented people, having reached and passed the limit of endurance, and overwhelmed with a sense of complete and utter failure, cried out in anguish:

"I can't carry this nation by myself! The load is far too heavy! If you are going to treat me like this, please kill me right now; it will be a kindness. Let me out of this impossible situation!" (Numbers 11:14, 15).

What Moses couldn't possibly know was that many, many years of wonderful service for God still lay ahead of him. Did God answer his prayer? No way!

It is a very serious thing when a believer—one who has placed his life in God's hand, is robbed of his desire to live. Yes, even for such as these something is missing.

ELIJAH

Look at a lone figure sitting forlornly under a broom bush out in the wilderness. He had traveled all day, fleeing for his life. Hot in pursuit, anxious to kill him, were the men sent by Queen Jezebel. Elijah had killed the wicked prophets of Baal—no small task, for 1 Kings 18:22 tells us that Baal had 450 prophets! The Lord gave special strength to Elijah (1 Kings 18:46), but now, fresh from the most dramatic scene one can possibly imagine, where he had been the divine instrument in the hands of God, Elijah wilts. He sprawls exhausted, emotionally and physically, totally unfit to meet the threats of the raging Jezebel. Listen to him as he prays that he might die: "I've had enough," he told the Lord. "Take away my life. I've got to die sometime, and it might as well be now" 1 Kings 19:4).

Although Elijah felt that he had been driven to banishment and obscurity—things were much too hot for him in the land of Israel—and although he wished to die, God was still not through with him. God deals with us in a much better way than we actually deserve. What if God were actually to take us at our word and grant us our foolish passionate requests? We might lose ourselves, as it were, like Elijah in a wilderness, but we are not lost to the watchful loving care and eye of the Lord when we are His children. For want of foresight we don't know how to pray as we ought, but God's grace is sufficient. His provision is enough to meet our every need. He *will* take care of us. He took care of Elijah, keeping him alive, feeding him by ravens, then by an angel, and then while he traveled in a maze through the desert for forty days without meat or food. God sustained and encouraged Elijah and in due time brought him out alive.

JONAH

Have you ever said, "I'd rather be dead than alive"? If so, you were only echoing what Jonah, the prophet who ran away from

God said at one time. God had given a difficult assignment to Jonah, but Jonah forgot that God is with us in these difficult places, and he took off in the opposite direction. Instead of going to Nineveh, he went down to the seacoast port of Joppa, where he found a ship leaving for Tarshish. He ended up inside the belly of a great fish after he had been thrown overboard into the raging sea by the ship's crew.

The interior of a great sea monster is a strange place to have a prayer meeting, but Jonah had a confrontation with God in the ocean's depths. Jonah said something very profound (which he later forgot). He said, "When I had lost all hope, I turned my thoughts once more to the Lord" (Jonah 2:7). Surely when we are plunged to the very pit of despair, we, like Jonah, must remember to turn our thoughts once more to the Lord. Can we not learn from Jonah's horrible experience that if we would not run away from God, if we would not take our thoughts off him to begin with, we wouldn't get into such trouble or feel "locked out of life," as Jonah put it?

The Lord ordered the fish to spit up Jonah on the beach, and it did. Then the Lord spoke to Jonah again: "Go to that great city, Nineveh," he said, "and warn them of their doom, as I told you to before!" (Jonah 3:1-2).

This time Jonah obeyed and returned to deliver God's message to wicked Nineveh. To his amazement and dismay he saw that vast city turn to God; revival swept through it and its extensive suburbs. But then—and it is so difficult to understand why—Jonah got very angry. The Bible says that when God saw that the inhabitants of the city stopped their evil ways, He abandoned his plan to destroy them (Jonah 3:10).

Instead of leaping for joy, praising and thanking God, what did Jonah do? He went outside the city, sat sulking under a gourd, and complained:

"This is exactly what I thought you'd do, Lord, when I was there in my own country and you first told me to come here. That's why I ran away to Tarshish. For I knew you were a gracious God, merciful, slow to get angry, and full of kindness: I knew how easily you could cancel your plans for destroying these people.

"Please kill me, Lord; I'd rather be dead than alive (when

nothing that I told them happens).

"Then the Lord said, 'Is it right to be angry about this'?" (Jonah 4:1-4).

But even while Jonah sat there moaning and feeling sorry for himself because his predictions hadn't come true and he felt like a fool, God was taking pity on him. When the leaves of the shelter he had erected to shade himself from the heat began to wither, the Lord arranged for a vine to grow up quickly and spread its broad leaves over Jonah's head to shade him. This made him comfortable and very grateful (Jonah 4:5, 6).

For the second time Jonah expresses the death wish (Jonah 4:8). The first time Jonah felt God had shattered his reputation as a prophet. He had prophesied judgment, and God had exercised mercy. Since his reputation was gone, Jonah concluded that it would be better to die than to live. There are those who believe that the second time, Jonah might have experienced something physical, such as sunstroke, which might have left him sick enough to wish to die.

God had to reprimand Jonah again and said, "Is it right for you to be angry because the plant died?"

" 'Yes,' Jonah said, 'it is; it is right for me to be angry enough to die!'

"Then the Lord said, 'You feel sorry for yourself when your shelter is destroyed, though you did no work to put it there, and it is, at best, short-lived. And why shouldn't I feel sorry for a great city like Nineveh with its 120,000 people in utter spiritual darkness' " (Jonah 4:9-10).

Moses, Elijah, and Jonah—three men, all mightily used by God, yet so much like us in our frailty and human weakness—so prone to complaining, feeling sorry for ourselves, indulging in self-pity, resentful even of God's grace and mercy.

THE BIBLE IS CONTEMPORARY

Thank God He has left us the biblical record. It's all there to help, instruct and to encourage us. The biographies of God's heroes are written for our needs today. The Bible is very contemporary. These men were God's heroes, but they were very human. We don't have to apologize for our humanness. As the well-known Gert Behanna, former alcoholic, whose story is told in *The*

Late Liz, once said, ''God must have thought an awful lot of us humans; after all, he came in the flesh!''

Just because they copped out on God along the line for a brief period of time, God didn't cop out on them. But how much better it is to learn the lessons from such as these so that we don't have to go through what they did. We don't have to long for death or contemplate suicide. There is a better way to cope with life's complexities.

It would be simplistic, unwise, unfair, and unrealistic to say that the thing that is missing in the lives of all those who commit suicide is a relationship with God through Jesus Christ. Such a blanket generalization is far too often thrown over what many consider ''the scandal of suicide.'' A generalization like that is most unkind to the memory of the person who took his own life, only adds to the hurt and heartache of the victim's family, and causes his friends needless distress. It relegates the suicide victim to hell, banished forever from the presence of God and loved ones who may have preceded him in death and others who will surely ultimately follow him in death.

Of course, it is distressing and disappointing when one who has professed faith in Christ takes his life with deliberate intent. Someone who wrote to the Billy Graham newspaper column, ''My Answer,'' asked whether a Christian who committed suicide could be saved? The writer stated that a wonderful Christian in her church had committed suicide and that it was a shock to everyone. The suicide victim was known to be a sweet, considerate person. It threw everyone in the church and raised many questions.

The answer is that only the Lord knows the circumstances surrounding the person's death.

I find Ben Haden's outlook on suicide a refreshing change from those who would sit so harshly in judgment upon the suicide victim. Mr. Haden says, and we agree, ''There's nothing that turns my stomach more than to see Christians who sit down and speculate on where someone driven to the point of suicide will spend eternity. That's up to *God . . .* it's *not* up to you or me.''[1]

The fact cannot be ignored, however, that there are those who do commit suicide who have not had a vital personal encounter with the living Christ. What is missing in their lives is a definite relationship to God through Christ.

THE APOSTLE PAUL

It was the Apostle Paul who said, "Christ lives in me. And the real life I now have within this body is a result of my trusting in the Son of God, who loved me and gave himself for me." (Galatians 2:20).

The Bible assures us that when we are willing to face our difficulties, committing our lives to God and then trusting Him to work out His perfect will in our lives, then we can be more than conquerers through Him who loved us. If there is one thing the Bible does make clear, it is the fact that we can expect trouble and problems in this life. No one is exempted from some degree of situational problems, painful illness, distressing loneliness, disabling handicaps, money problems, stormy love affairs, difficult interpersonal relationships, domestic difficulties, old age, or anxiety in one form or another.

We all need a large "cope-scope"! Acknowledging our own weakness and inability to cope is not a sign of weakness. In fact, it is a good thing to turn to God and say, "Look, this is more than I can take. I simply don't understand everything that's happening to me and the situation in the world around me. It all appears utterly futile and hopeless. What's the use? If You've got any solutions and can help me cope, then, Lord, I'm more than willing to exchange my weakness for Your strength." The Apostle Paul could say in his time of trauma and weakness, "I can do all things through Christ which strengtheneth me" (Philippians 4:13, *KJV*).

Hardship and suffering were not foreign to Paul. Prior to making the above statement he had said, "I have learned how to get along happily whether I have much or little. I know how to live on almost nothing or with everything. I have learned the secret of contentment in every situation, whether it be a full stomach or hunger, plenty or want" (Philippians 4:11, 12). He knew what it was to be in bonds and imprisoned. Deprivation, sickness, persecution, loneliness—all of these and more were within his experience. What was he saying? Only that whatever the circumstances, he could handle them, because he transferred the weight of them all to God, trusting Him to work out His perfect will in His life. It was Christ Who strengthened him. In the power of His might, Paul said he could endure (Ephesians 6:10).

To young Timothy, his son in the faith, he could wisely say from practical experience that it is possible to be strengthened with might by God's Spirit working in the inner man, whose strength comes from the grace that is in Christ Jesus (2 Timothy 2:1). The manner in which he stated this indicated a present and continued supply of strength that made him equal to whatever confronted him.

These were not just petty, pious-sounding words conjured up by a man with a unique talent for expressing himself well. Here was a man who had been the most aggressive and influential enemy of the early Church. He was its biggest persecutor. He had been on both sides of the fence—against Christ and then all-out for him. His was as complex a personality as one can meet within the pages of the Bible. He was both conservative and radical, venturesome and cautious. He possessed an excess of zeal, which was bent on destroying every vestige of Christianity until he had an amazing confrontation with Christ on the road to Damascus. Paul was the most difficult kind of man to convert; therefore, if you think you are an impossible breed, utterly beyond the reach of the help of God through Christ, then a long look at the Apostle Paul is in order for you.

SATAN'S GATEWAY TO DEFEAT

If Paul's life could be salvaged, so can yours. It has been said that suicide is Satan's gateway to defeat, but Christ is the only "Door" to freedom and victory! Paul learned this as he faced the harassment of those who opposed Christ just as he himself had once done. Weariness and pain, hunger and thirst, cold and nakedness, beatings and imprisonments, stoning and shipwreck, perils on land and sea, were his missionary experience (2 Corinthians 11:23-28). How did he react? Did he wish to die? Did he seek the door of escape through suicide? He did not. He lived through all of this, not just passively enduring what was happening to him but actually glorying in his infirmities so that the power of Christ might rest upon him (2 Corinthians 12:9). Paul could say, "I will suffer, I will bear reproach, I will be bold."

Paul was writing to those who were being persecuted for naming themselves Christians. His counsel to them was to people who were enduring great trouble, whose very lives were often in danger. So when he said, "Whatever happens, dear friends, be glad in the Lord" (Philippians 3:1), he was actually speaking to those whose situation looked anything but promising. Was there much to be glad about? Wasn't everything pretty hopeless? Yes, things were grim. Paul reminded them, "Put [your] trust and hope in Christ alone . . . This is the only way to experience His mighty power on your behalf" (Philippians 3:7).

Did Paul ever express the death wish? Did the thought of dying enter into his thinking? It did, but not exactly in the way of one who contemplates suicide, it may be said with reasonable certainty. Paul expressed it like this: "I am in a strait betwixt two, having a desire to depart, and to be with Christ; which is far better: nevertheless to abide in the flesh is more needful for you" (Philippians 1:23-24, *KJV*). Paul was saying that living means opportunities for Christ, and dying—well, that's better yet! But if living will give me more opportunities to win people to Christ, then I really don't know which is better, to live or die. Sometimes I want to live and at other times I don't, for I long to go and be with Christ. How much happier for me than being here! But the fact is that I can be of more help to you by staying. Yes, I am still needed down here and so I feel certain I will be staying on earth a little longer, to help you grow and become happy in your faith (Philippians 1:21-25).

Paul definitely looked forward to death as a release from life's vicissitudes, but as long as he was in the land of the living he would show himself to be a channel of God's grace and great love. The thing that Paul had going for him that many who take their own lives apparently do not possess in adequate measure was a total self-lessness. His focus was on Christ and the giving of His life to secure salvation and the rewards and beauties of heaven for him and all those who would acknowledge and receive Him.

HOW TO KEEP ON "KEEPING ON"

Paul was able to look away from his own discomforts, the threats on his life, the physical infirmity that he described as "a thorn in the flesh," and the uncertainties that surrounded his existence, and in so doing he could "keep on keeping on." He described life as a race in which a good runner exerts every bit of physical energy to win; life was a battle in which the good soldier puts on that which equips him to fight a good fight.

But always his dependency was upon Christ, and he urged his hearers to keep their eyes likewise on Jesus. My hope in Christ is steadfast, Paul could say, and my consolation comes from Him.

This was no idle boast or trumped up spiritualizing. He was speaking from experience—life was tough, a real battle, a long difficult race with many obstacles thrown in the way. There were hurdles to overcome and the enemy to fight. To endure, a man had to have a strategy and inner fortification.

It was of immense help when others were for him, not working against him, Paul had discovered; and so he cautioned against all sorts of things that we can do unthinkingly or deliberately that impede our own or others' progress in life. We are to love each other and show it. We are patiently and kindly to help those who are going through difficult times. Forgive each other and comfort one another, Paul strongly advised. The reason? If a person is going through great anguish and grief, if the problems loom high, we are not to add to his affliction. Paul said that unless a person receives help from others that can instill some hope within him, he may be "swallowed up with overmuch sorrow" (2 Corinthians 2:7, *KJV*).

Unless we are willing to do this, Satan will get the advantage. Those are not my words; again they come from Paul (2 Corinthians 2:11). Bitterness and discouragement can so overtake one that unless we who are strong in the Lord and aware of the adversary's tactics come to the rescue of one who is overburdened with life's complexities, there is great danger that such a person will not recover but, succumb to despair. It is in these moments that mental derangement can take over to the extent that even a committed Christian can commit suicide.

Suicide has long been a taboo subject that stigmatizes not only the victim but the survivors as well. The act of self-destruction raises vital questions: "Why? Where have I failed?" It is an affront to those who remain, as they anxiously ask, "How can I now face people? What will others think?"

Therefore, those of us who are Christians, when confronted with the fact of suicide—when someone we know has killed himself, or even when we hear of someone we do not know personally who has done this dread thing—it is not our prerogative to sit around speculating on the whys and wherefores. Instead, we must exercise great wisdom, tact, and understanding love that says, "Look, I love you. I don't understand, but I want to be understanding. Your loved one is gone; we entrust him to God's tender mercy. Now what can I do to help you?" Most often just being there, available with love, a comforting arm around the shoulder, and a listening ear will help to ease the pain of the loss and the agony of disturbing questions.

RECOGNIZE THAT LIFE IS A GIFT OF GOD

Life is to be treasured. How sad when someone despairs of its wonderful possibilities and is driven to suicide. Life is a gift of God, but it becomes really meaningful when love enters the picture. God's great gift to mankind was personified in His Gift of Love, Jesus. When you show others His Gift of Love, then you give them the greatest gift of all.

If you really want to do something for the world or for someone who has just experienced a loss of a loved one through suicide or for someone who has attempted to take his life but failed, then the thing to do is to reach out with *love*—not the sentimental wishy-washy false brand of giving that poses as love, but genuine *loving* that involves giving of yourself.

---

1. Ben Haden, Rebel to Rebel (Miami: Logo, 1971).

Discouragement is a satanic tool that seems
to fit my disposition very well.

*Jim Elliott, martyred missionary to the
Auca Indians in Ecuador, from his journal* [1]

10

Suicide: A Satanic Tool

The devil, our sworn enemy, is a "murderer from the beginning" according to John's gospel (John 8:44). It is plain to see why suicide is the second leading cause of death among young people between fifteen and twenty-four years of age. If Satan succeeds in destroying the younger generation, he has accomplished a mighty aim. The devil is happiest when he sees that he can destroy one of God's children. It was Jim Elliott, martyred missionary to Ecuador, who wrote in his diary, "Discouragement is a Satanic tool that seems to fit my disposition very well."

The disciple Peter, who knew what it was to be hounded by Satan, said, "Be careful—watch out for attacks from Satan, your great enemy. He prowls around like a hungry, roaring lion, looking for some victim to tear apart. Stand firm when he attacks. Trust the Lord" (1 Peter 5:8-9).

The recognition then must come that each one of us is important to God. It is Satan who is planting seeds of mistrust and doubt in our thinking. Count it a joy and a privilege to be attacked, but don't succumb to the battle. Fight it. Suffer through it. Peter said, "After you have suffered a little while, our God, who is full of kindness through Christ, will give you his eternal glory. He personally will come and pick you up, and set you firmly in place, and make you stronger than ever. To him be all power" (1 Peter 5:10-11).

A letter writer asked whether God would get tired of hearing her call out to Him. The answer to that is an emphatic *no.* It is unbelief, pitting circumstances between itself and God, that causes doubt and the feeling that Jesus is not there. We are not to count on our feelings, they fluctuate; we are to rest on *the fact* that Jesus does exist, He does come into our hearts when we invite Him, and we do not need constantly to be inviting Him in when He is already there. We need to accept the fact of His abiding presence.

LET NOT YOUR HEART BE TROUBLED

The resources at our disposal are unbelievable. God, the Creator of the universe, is big enough to create and take care of the world and still be interested in you and in me as individual persons.

When Jesus was talking to His disciples after the Last Supper, He told them some of the things that were going to happen to Him. He told them that He was going to be leaving them. It broke their hearts. No wonder they were saddened. It showed on their faces. And that's when He said, "Let not your heart be troubled. You are trusting God, now trust in me" (John 14:1). Jesus made that statement to His disciples at a crucial moment in their lives. They were almost petrified with fear. Desperate despondency, darkest doubt filled their minds. Jesus looked at those anxious disciples, just as He still perceives the inner heart of people today. Jesus knows our souls in adversity. He knows every question, every doubt that plagues your thoughts. Every wound that inwardly bleeds is known to Him. There is no way you can escape from His all-seeing eye. The psalmist knew that. He said, "He that keepeth thee will not slumber. Behold. . . . He shall neither slumber nor sleep" (Psalm 121:3-4 *KJV*).

Those are words for you, too. For one who is contemplating suicide, who wishes to escape the world about him with its problems and difficult people, Jesus is speaking those words to you also. It is as if He is saying, "If you have invited me into your heart, then let your mind rest itself on that, even though circumstances around you are disturbing and upsetting." His words are meant to convey the idea that we are not to be in a state of confusion or hurry. Rest on Him. Be sensible. Patient. Keep possession of your soul and your mind even though you can't keep anything else. You may lose your job, a loved one may have died, someone may have slandered your name. Whatever is causing you such turmoil, Jesus is saying, *"Believe in God and believe in me. Don't be afraid."*

The happiness of heaven is our eventual destination when we are believers. Although all else around us may seem to fall apart and people may fail us (as they will surely do), Jesus that day set before

His disciples the indisputable fact that He was going away to heaven to prepare a place for them and for all those who put their trust in Him. Thomas, remember him? He was called doubting Thomas. He had some questions for Jesus. Jesus answered them. (You can read all about it in the fourteenth chapter of John). Jesus said, "I am not making up this answer to your question. It is the answer given by the Father who sent me" (John 14:24b).

Grasp hold of the reality of God and don't let go. It is this that will energize and fortify you against every onslaught of Satan, who would seek to destroy you and rob you of your faith. Thank God you are being hounded. Struggle can only make you more patient, sensitive, and godlike when, through God's strength and power, you overcome it.

Remember Job? Everything that meant anything to him had been destroyed, swept away, demolished—even his children. But can't you see him lifting his boil-covered arm to heaven and shouting, "Though he slay me, yet will I trust in him" (Job 13: 15a, *KJV*)?

Stop looking for God to wave some magical wand that will give you all the answers to your questions and remove all the obstacles and problems. Instead, act on your faith, weak as it may be, and then watch God move in response to your first feeble steps for Him. Your destiny and the outcome of this world are terribly important to God. He thought so much of it that He sent His Son Jesus into the world to save it.

We need to praise God more. Our problems persist as long as we bask in them, feeling sorry for ourselves, all turned inward. In Psalm 56, David complains of his enemies; then, with a resounding note of triumph, he declares emphatically, "In God have I put my trust; I will not be afraid of what man can do to me" (Psalm 56:11, *KJV*).

"This one thing I know," David shouts, "God is for me! I am trusting God—oh, praise His promises" (Psalm 56:9, 10)! Then he adds, "Thank you, Lord, for Your help" (vs. 12b). Would the world around you doubt God less if they saw you praising Him more?

Matthew Henry said, "Praising and blessing God is work that is never out of season. Nothing better prepares the mind for receiving the Holy Spirit than holy joy and praise. Fears are silenced, sorrows sweetened, and hopes kept up.''

"Believe in God," said Jesus. "That doesn't mean protection, and it doesn't mean safety; it doesn't mean security, and it doesn't mean immunity from suffering and conflict," wrote J. Wallace Hamilton. God is not a security blanket. He is much more than that.

SOMETIMES IT HELPS TO CRY

There is nothing wrong with tears. One need not be ashamed of shedding them. Many were spilled in the Bible, particularly by the writer of the Psalms. Always, however, the God of all comfort was there with reassurance. At one point David, in great turmoil, cries out, "You have collected all my tears and preserved them in your bottle! You have recorded every one in your book" (Psalm 56:8).

David, however, was unwilling to "throw in the towel." he may have wept, but he knew God could be depended upon to understand what those tears were all about. David didn't hang up his harp on the willow trees; he didn't unstring it and lay it aside: He kept it and himself right in tune by singing God's praises. He encouraged himself in God; he did not look to people or the circumstances surrounding him. It was God's providence, His power and promises, that David trusted in. God was his confidence.

Just as the blood of the saints, spilled through the years as they have suffered for the cause of Christ, is precious to the Lord, so too are the tears we shed as we call out to Him not wasted. They are not lost to God. The tears of God's people are bottled up and sealed among God's treasures. God will reckon with those who have caused tears to come from His people's eyes. Prayer and tears, David is telling us, are good weapons for God's people as we face that which shakes us to the very roots of our faith.

In many places throughout the Bible we read of God's saying, "I have seen thy tears." We, like the biblical saints who cried to the Lord, need to remember that God answered and delivered His people then from unbelievably harsh circumstances and that He has been doing this down through all the intervening centuries. He is not a God of caprice, answering then and refusing now!

God doesn't hand out medals to those who do not weep! Weeping is a very valid and normal emotion—even for men. God made you with a sensitive nature and the capacity to feel and experience emotions and grief. Remember, the Bible says that even ''Jesus wept.'' That happens to be the shortest verse in the Bible. Another short verse is ''God is love.'' Life will be strong and rich and full of meaning in direct proportion to your willingness to release your capacity to love on the world and those with whom you come in contact. We are to be walking love to each other.

The child who said to his mother, ''I want a God with a face on,'' was not asking for the impossible. He was only expressing what mankind has always sought after—reality. He wanted something definite, something tangible. He wanted a *someone* for a God, not a something.

---

1. Elisabeth Elliot, *Shadow of The Almighty*, (New York: Harper & Row, 1958).

"Anyone in the emotional vicinity
of the suicidal person, including
family members, clergymen, physicians,
therapists, and friends, is in a position
to prevent a tragic and wasteful death." [1]
Dr. Paul W. Pretzel

11

What Can Be Done About the Growing Problem of Suicide?

It is a commonly held belief by those working in the field of suicidology that most suicides can be prevented. When you talk with those who have attempted suicide, the family members of some who have succeeded, and the therapists who deal with it, you come away recognizing that predicting who will and who won't commit suicide is extremely difficult, if not impossible. Statistics and studies are useful, but the problem remains highly personal and exceedingly complex. Nevertheless, it is good for us to shore ourselves up with as much knowledge as possible about suicide so that if we can be a "gatekeeper" to anyone, we will be responsive *and* responsible.

LEGACY FROM THE DEAD

Can we, the living, take a legacy from the suicidal dead? Hopefully, yes.

Dr. Paul Pretzel, a practicing clinical psychologist, and assistant professor in the Psychology Department of California State University in Los Angeles, emphasizes in his book *Understanding and Counseling The Suicidal Person* that short-term, active, crisis intervention is nearly always effective for one caught in the suicidal crisis. The temporary failure of these individuals to cope simply means that in their cry for help—and most suicides give plenty of advance warning clues—they are reaching out for help and hope.

BE AWARE OF SUICIDAL GESTURING

Take every threat of suicide seriously. Dr. Calvin J. Frederick, psychologist with the National Institute of Mental Health's Center for studies of Crime and Delinquency, states: ". . . suicide is perceptible, predictable and preventable . . ." Suicide prevention centers train their workers to be alert to suicidal gesturing.

Some of those "gestures" or signals would be withdrawal into isolation, outright threats to commit suicide, writing a will and getting business affairs in order, or making a point of saying "Good-bye" or "If I see you again . . ." Giving away possessions is another clue. There are also blatant signs, like the child who tells you, "You won't have to be bothered with me much longer."

Any *significant* change in personality or behavior would be a warning sign. If a fairly happy adolescent suddenly becomes quiet or morose, or if a usually quiet teenager becomes manic in behavior, it could be a sign.

Be aware of mental depression. This is terribly important. Physical manifestations like sleeplessness, loss of appetite, weight loss, headache, general aches and pains as well as psychological symptoms like lethargy, crying, apathy and an inability to concentrate—these are all danger signs. Dr. Pretzel says these are people "hungry for human contact and overly grateful for any small bit that one would give him." [2]

GESTURES, SIGNALS, SIGNS, SUICIDAL COMMUNICATION: MISSED, IGNORED OR MISINTERPRETED

Careful investigation after a suicide and conversations with loved ones and friends reveals many clear attempts at communication which have been missed, ignored or misinterpreted by those closest to the suicide.

The question is in order: Why? Why, when the communications are so clear in retrospect, are they not received at the time they are given?

One possible answer is that we all have psychological defenses which can go into operation without our really being aware of it. Who wants to admit that someone you care about and for whom you may have a responsibility is feeling suicidal? Suicide is the whispered word; the taboo topic; and so we skirt the issue everytime it rears its ugly head, we don't want involvement in anything that spooky; weird, risky, or morbid. We tell ourselves the individual is only trying to get some sympathy, or gain some attention, or make us feel sorry for him. Indeed! Precisely!

DENIAL, RATIONALIZATION, REACTING AGGRESSIVELY

Many individuals have admitted that they repressed the communication that came to them from a suicide. That is another psychological defense whereby we simply deny at the time we hear an individual saying something we really don't like to hear. Or we have heard of people responding to a suicide's cry for help by stating, "Now you know you don't really mean that." Like the lonely elderly person who says, "I am getting nowhere on my own. I need help. I would be better off dead." Or the child who tells her father, "I'm going to run away," and the daddy responds by saying, "Go ahead . . ." and laughs. Later she comes to him again and says, "You don't love me. I'll eat my aspirin." And she does just that. Discovered in time, her stomach was pumped. The parents were warned, "This may have been a deliberate suicide attempt." But they discarded the idea: "She was just trying to get attention."

One may react aggressively also. Many people will become angry upon hearing a suicidal hint or threat, as if to say the suicidal victim has no right in exposing the listener to such feelings of anxiety and discomfort. [3]

It is not denied that selfish motives are frequently involved in a suicide attempt—feelings of self-pity, strong narcissistic tendencies, self-love, i.e., *excessive* interest in one's self. Yet even such as these do need help. It is shocking that most preventable suicide is for many a tragically childish act, and indeed a way of seeking attention or sympathy.

E.S. Schneidman in *Essays in Self-Destruction* [4] really lays it on the line in his observation that "The suicidal person places his psychological skeleton in the survivor's closet." In so doing, the suicide derives a sadistic sort of satisfaction (while living) from the thought that he can make those who hurt him or denied him in some way, whether it was real or imagined, live with the memory for the rest of their lives that they were, in fact, the cause of his killing himself. He *wants* them to live with guilt, shame, and self-blame.

So pre-suicidal communications and conversations, as well as suicide notes, give many clues as to the "why" of suicide. And there are those who take their own lives who are selfish manipulative type individuals who, when they cannot have their own way, will resort to self-murder or make an attempt upon their own lives to gain attention and sympathy. Many such persons take just enough drugs, for example, to put themselves into a stupor and will time their attempts to coincide with someone's coming home from work or an expected visit of a friend or family member. They know this will be discovered "in time." Sometimes, however, this is not the case, and in their stupified condition they may go on to take more drugs, forgetting the actual count, and end up a suicide statistic. Their little scheme has backfired, and death is the result. It is felt that this happens in *many* instances.

Still, such as these are to be pitied. Christian love requires that we *not* withhold love even from those who are unlovable for whatever reason. We should do what we can to help them and to secure professional help to see them through their crisis times.

Someone asks, "But would a Christian do that?" Is it possible for a Christian to be guilty of resorting to such means to get attention or to try to regain back a lost love on a marriage that has gone completely sour, or a love relationship before marriage? The answer is yes. An editorial in the magazine *Christianity Today* stated, "While a strong Christian commitment tends to reduce the possibility of suicide, it does not eliminate it." [5] These are often individuals who cannot get away from themselves. This is one of the contributing causes to their sour love relationship. Unless they accept help and are willing to heed the advice of others, they may successfully destroy themselves, if not through suicide then through living a life all distorted by selfish values and reasoning that is turned inward, out of focus, and off balance. In the process they will reach out with unseen tentacles to ensnare family members and friends. Many husbands, wives, children, and friends are made to suffer by the actions of such as these.

Sometimes the victims themselves are unsuspecting, so successful is the suicidal individual at playing his or her "game." Others are aware of the individual's motives but feel trapped, helpless to do anything about the situation. There are many marriages, for example, that are being held together by the thinnest of threads—the threat of "I'll kill myself if you leave me." To prove his or her intent, the individual will sometimes make such an attempt. "Now," she thinks with satisfaction, "he'll know I mean business. He won't leave me."

Young people play the same sort of dangerous "game" in their own manipulative ways. It is granted that many such pleas and "games" are selfish in nature. Still, they should *never* be regarded lightly. Threats turn into action. A passive declaration of "I wish I were dead" becomes an act. Selfish, childish, impulsive, or real without false motives—whatever names are attached to the act, it is sad, unnecessary, and an affront to God, one's family, the community, and society in general. The philosopher Immanuel Kant was correct when he said that suicide is an insult to humanity.

IMMOBILIZATION AND FEAR OF INVOLVEMENT

For fear of invading another's privacy, many people fail to respond to the suicidal gesture. There is a form of immobilization which has the effect of paralyzing a person's response. Often this is a result of not really knowing how to respond and the fear of involvement and saying the wrong thing. An individual will change the subject of conversation, or avoid the topic and profess interest in something or someone. When someone reaches out in a suicidal gesture with a cry for help, Dr. Pretzel so wisely states, "They are not needing a lifelong commitment, but only the willingness from a concerned person to become actively involved for a short period of time." [6] Remember, most suicidal crises are relatively short-lived. Isn't it a small price to pay to be involved if a life can be saved?

Ann Landers column told the horrifying account of a woman teetering on a window ledge, threatening to kill herself. Someone in the crowd below shouted, "Jump. Nobody gives a damn." She jumped!

The writer of the letter revealed how she very nearly did the same thing at one time in her life, "but I was lucky enough to have someone around who DID give a damn. My heart aches for that man who told her to jump. There is something tragic about a person who is so uncaring. I wonder what happened in *his* life that made him that way . . ."

She went on to call attention to the thousands of heartbreaking and untimely deaths through suicide that occur every day. Then there are deaths that don't seem to matter much. "But, like John Donne, I believe 'each man's death diminishes me.' I thank God every day that when I teetered on the ledge someone was near to save me.''

The reason that a suicidal person is making his communication is for the purpose of inviting concern and inquiry into the state of his life, and if this concern is not manifested, the suicidal person rightly experiences this as a rejection and as a lack of caring. The normal effect of this is to encourage him in his suicidal thinking. 7

PERSONAL PRISONS

To speak of one's fears and problems takes some of the potency away. Someone has stated that fear is not the thing that is so terrifying, but it is the personal prison we build for ourselves.

We feel we have to put on a good front; we must appear respectable; we become geniuses at erecting facades. Inside we are raw and bleeding; we mistakenly think people would find us totally unacceptable if they only knew. We conceal our anger, our disappointment, our frustrations, our hurts. And some end up suicide statistics.

THE RISK OF DESENSITIZING OTHERS

Someone reading this may have been seeing himself or herself in this chapter. There is danger in chronic suicide gestures whereby we, like the shepherd boy who cried "Wolf" too often, will find people no longer responding. Our cries for help have come too often; the effect has been to minimize the importance of our situation in the eyes and ears of significant people who could and would help. It's sort of like emotional blackmail; an unpleasant way of intimidating others.

OTHERS WHO ARE SUICIDE RISKS

It should be emphasized that alcoholics and drug-abusers count for a disproportionate number of suicides, and suicide rates are high among widows, divorced people, gamblers, unwed teenage mothers, the recently unemployed, and the bankrupt. Watch for ''gestures'' from such as these.

SUICIDE TIMING

There is a myth that once a suicidal crisis is over, it won't reoccur. Available documentation shows that most suicides occur within about three months following the beginning of "improvement," when the individual has regained the energy to put his still morbid thoughts and feelings into effect again.

It may come as a surprise to some, but traditionally happy events may also trigger suicide attempts. It is acknowledged that suicides increase at Christmas. Why? Because the holiday happiness of others only emphasizes the victim's loneliness. And loneliness is now called the nation's #1 disease.

A newspaper headline carries the disturbing announcement that IN THE SPRING A YOUNG MAN'S FANCY OFTEN TURNS TO SUICIDE. When spring comes, the suicide rate goes up. Life comes back to the earth ever so gently, and then folks do themselves in in greater numbers than at any other time of the year. In spring, as the old saying goes, a young man's fancy lightly turns to thoughts of death. The world is luscious. Crocuses come, and daffodils—and death.

PRIMARY PREVENTION

If you notice suicidal gestures or signs in anyone, anyplace, the first and most important rule in such instances is DO SOMETHING.

> Get help—a doctor, psychiatrist, psychologist, therapist, a friend, a family member, a pastor, priest or chaplain. Get the person to a hospital, mental health clinic, suicide prevention center or crisis intervention center right away.

Never assume that the crisis is over just because the person says it is or seems to feel and act more like his normal self.

GIVE FRIENDSHIP. GIVE LOVE, ACCEPTANCE, AND SHOW THAT YOU CARE. COMMUNICATE.

GET THE SUICIDAL PERSON TO TALK. Encourage expression of feelings. Accentuate the positive aspects of living. Remind the person of those who would be left behind, bereaved, saddened, hurt and suffer loss if he carried out his plan.

DON'T MAKE MORAL JUDGMENTS. Concentrate on talking about things that will give him or her a reason and a will to live.

DON'T GET INVOLVED IN LIFE VERSUS DEATH ARGUMENTS. Your goal should be to restore the person's feelings of self-worth and dignity.

ACT. TAKE CHARGE. Take pills away, take a gun away—whatever potentially lethal weapon the person may have been threatening to use. Involve the immediate help of others.

SECONDARY INTERVENTION

Suicidal behavior can be understood as a manifestation of the person's need for some basic change in his life. Dr. Pretzel underscores this and the fact that if things do *not* change, the chance of further suicidal behavior is very high. The nature and quality of the actions that are taken after a suicidal hint, threat, or attempt, therefore, will often spell the difference between life and death. Yet, many suicidal indications are not followed up by supposedly concerned people who are in touch with the distressed person. [8]

Adequate follow-up and a continuity is vital for the rehabilitation of a suicidal person. Sometimes what the suicidal person wants is not feasible (a dead wife or husband cannot be revived; sometimes a broken love relationship cannot be restored, etc.), but efforts must be made to create some kind of support plan which will provide the individual with a measure of security and hope for the immediate present and the future.

I believe, too, that the role of the counselor trained in treating the suicidal individual is an essential part of recovery. In no way would I minimize the help to be received from psychologists, psychiatrists, and therapists, who can delve into the suicidal person's complex physical and psychological makeup. I also believe that faith and hope belong together, and the same things that are the objects of our hope are the objects of our faith. Permit me, therefore, to express my convictions that there is a way out of the suicidal person's dilemma.

---

1. Paul W. Pretzel, *Understanding and Counseling the Suicidal Person* (Nashville, Tenn.: Abingdon Press, 1972).

2. Ibid., p. 89.

3. Ibid., p. 94.

4. E.S. Schneidman, *Essays in Self-Destruction* (New York: International Science Press, 1967).

5. "Up from Suicide" (editorial), *Christianity Today* (June 9, 1972).

6. Paul W. Pretzel, p. 95.

7. Ibid., p. 94, 95.

8. Ibid., p. 120.

Faith demonstrates to the eye of the mind
the reality of those things that cannot be
discerned by the eye of the body.
Faith is believing where we cannot see,
trusting in Christ beyond the horizon,
believing His goodness beyond our
sight, trusting His word against the optic nerve.
J. Wallace Hamilton
What About Tomorrow? [1]

12

Go to the Top for Help

The final act of suicide is basically a
resolution, a movement, perceived as the
only possible one, out of a life situation felt
to be unbearable by one of low sense of
competence, with hope extinguished.
Maurice L. Farber,
The Theory of Suicide [2]

An anonymous article in *These Times* magazine, written by a
successful high school science teacher who loved his work, who
was continually receiving salary raises and was liked and respected
by students and colleagues yet was plagued by thoughts of wanting
to kill himself, has as its title "Go to the Top for Help." [3] The
author admits that "Satan had me by the nose, leading me around,
and I didn't even know it." Life became for him "a living hell,"
but "death scared me because I had no real idea what lay beyond
life." He came to the conclusion that he wanted out of life regardless of whom he hurt and regardless of what lay beyond the other
side of death.

The writer's judgment is that the mental anguish that induces
suicidal thoughts becomes emotional illness. Mental pain, like
physical pain, can become so unbearable that in desperation the
person is driven to a remedy so drastic that he destroys all in trying
to save part. In his anguish, one fateful night, he walked over to a

window, stared out at the bright moon and in a demanding voice shouted, ''God, Jesus, or whoever You are! If You're really out there! If You're real and alive. If You can save me, You'd better do it in the next five minutes or forget about it!'' He dropped to his knees and started to cry as he thought of the terrible things he'd done in his life and felt the urge to confess them, seeking forgiveness.

He describes what happened like this:

''An unknown, yet exhilarating, feeling settled over me, like I had been covered with a blanket of love. I cannot describe exactly how I felt, but perhaps the feeling can be best expressed in the words of a teenager who having just been converted ran up to me and shouted, 'I've got God! I've got God!' That's somewhat like I felt, I had God, or maybe more correctly, He had me. After years and years of wandering, ignoring, guessing, doubting, and playing games, God was alive and real to me! I got up, weak from emotional exhaustion but strong with joy and hope, climbed back into bed and slept peacefully the rest of the night.

''The Bible says that faith comes from hearing and hearing from the word of God (Romans 10:17). During the next few days God began to develop my faith in Him and reveal to me just what had happened on the night I almost took my life. He guided me to particular passages in the Scriptures. I had not read the Bible for a long, long time. I didn't know where to begin. All I knew was that I should begin. I thumbed through its pages at random. Providentially I stopped at Psalm 40 and read: 'I waited patiently for God to help me; then he listened and heard my cry. He lifted me out of the pit of despair, out from the bog and the mire, and set my feet on a hard, firm path and steadied me as I walked along. He has given me a new song to sing.' (Psalm 40:1-3).

''I couldn't believe my eyes. The next told exactly what God had done for me—with one big exception. The man who wrote this psalm had waited patiently for God to help him. But not me! In my sin and pride I had demanded a reply from God right on the spot. Even so, God in His great love had listened. He had heard my cry for help. He had saved me. What a God! Again I flipped the pages, this time stopping at Psalm 139. My eyes fell on verse 7: 'I can *never* be lost to your Spirit! I can *never* get away from my God! If I go up to heaven, you are there: if I go down to the place of the dead, you are there' (Psalm 139:7-8).

"Once more God revealed to me through His Word the depths of His concern for me. A few days before I had almost taken my life, with Satan standing there ready to yank me into eternity with him, when the Lord intervened and pulled me back to safety. The fellow who wrote these words really knew what he was talking about. God is everywhere!"

MAN-SIZED PROBLEMS REQUIRE GOD-SIZED SOLUTIONS

The author concludes the telling of his experience by stating, "I do not know exactly why God saved me from myself . . . but He did, and I'm mighty thankful . . . Man-sized problems require God-sized solutions. Go to the top for help."

To those who say, "I am so sick of life sometimes I wonder what I am living for. I wish someone would kill me. I wish someone would put me in a cellar and throw away the key. I want to be happy and have something to live for. Can you help me?" Our answer is exactly what the science teacher who wanted out of life prescribed: Go to the top for help.

Sylvia Plath, a brilliant young successful writer, wanted out of this life also. As one views the suicide scene, taking into account those who have taken their own lives, it comes as a shock to discover how many talented, brilliant, and successful people end up taking their own lives. It gives credence to a fact that Christianity has long expounded, that success in and of itself, and possessions, cannot and do not make a person happy. One could point, for example, to the late Marilyn Monroe and other well-known (in their time) artists, politicians, writers, and creative people who have despaired of living when they discovered a final nothingness that existed in their creative worlds. Self-destruction among highly creative people is not rare.

Alvarez, in his study on suicide, takes the reader through a journey where one views the act of suicide as the end of a long experience, an emptiness so isolated and violent as to make life into such a paper-thin reality of hopelessness that the individual finally surrenders. He describes the final suicide act of Sylvia Plath, who was his friend.

Miss Plath herself wrote a fictionalized account of her struggle with herself and the events in her life, one of which was the time she went into the cellar of their home, crawled into the darkest, most inaccessible place she could find, carrying with her a tall glass of water and fifty sleeping pills that she'd taken from her mother's bureau drawer, and pushed "heavy, dust-covered logs across the hole mouth. The dark felt thick as velvet, I reached for the glass and the bottle, and carefully, on my knees, with bent head, crawled to the farthest wall . . . I unscrewed the bottle of pills and started taking them swiftly, between gulps of water, one by one by one." [4] But that was not to be the end of Sylvia Plath. Some time later, she was discovered and miraculously survived that first suicide attempt.

When I read the letter from the young person stating he wished he could crawl into a cellar and die, I immediately thought of Sylvia Plath's experience—an experience that resulted in her spending a great amount of time in and out of hospitals and institutions where she was kept for psychotherapy and shock treatment. She described it as "A time of darkness, despair, disillusion—so black only as the inferno of the human mind can be—symbolic death and numb shock—then the painful agony of slow rebirth and psychic regeneration." [5]

Later—much later—she was to end her own life successfully in a London flat by turning all the gas jets on and putting her head on the oven door. Alvarez believes this was a final desperate "cry for help" that fatally misfired. He believes that she expected to be found in time, but "her calculations went wrong and she lost." He says "her vision was blinkered by depression and illness." He feels "she was an enormously gifted poet whose death came carelessly, by mistake and too soon." [6]

In a world that is becoming increasingly superficial and artificial, when one does not go to the top for help or acknowledge that there is Someone at the top Who can give help and hope, then suicide seems far more desirable than does living a life of pretense in hopelessness.

THOSE "AT-THE-END-OF-THE-ROPE" FEELINGS

Of the many poems Ogden Nash wrote, one was entitled "Prayer at the End of a Rope." There have been many individuals who have had that "at-the-end-of-the-rope" feeling, who, in their despair, have called out to God in prayer and have been wonderously comforted and helped.

WHAT IS FAITH?

Look at the eleventh chapter of Hebrews. There you will find what is often referred to as "the roll call of faith" chapter. These are people who knew what it was to have the friendship of God and much more. There, faith is defined, as the writer of the book asks the question so many others ask, "What is faith? It is the confident assurance that something we want is going to happen. It is the certainty that what we hope for is waiting for us, even though we cannot see it up ahead. Men of God in days of old were famous for their faith" (Hebrews 11:1-2).

Here we are introduced to Abel, Enoch, Noah, Abraham, Isaac, Jacob, Sarah, Joseph, Moses, Rahab the harlot, Gideon, Barak, Samson, Jephthah, David, and Samuel, and mention is made of "all the other prophets" (men who possessed faith).

The triumphs of faith in the lives of Hebrew heroes and heroins, is powerful evidence that faith is something that is intensely practical. Faith is "taking God at His word." Faith is "accepting as true what God has revealed." When the Bible says that "faith is *assurance* of things hoped for," it must be understood that this "assurance" rests on divine promises. This is not mere speculation or frothy sentiment. Faith to be genuine will act with absolute confidence upon the reality of God as revealed by His Word and the conviction in one's inner spirit.

Faith can have as its starting point the fact that the visible world points to an invisible Creator. "By faith—by believing God—we know that the world and the stars—in fact, all things—were made at God's command; and that they were all made from things that can't be seen" (Hebrews 11:3). The first exercise of faith, then, it would appear from Chapter 11 of Hebrews, which deals so specifically with faith, is to accept the fact of creation and its Creator.

So you cannot see beyond today. Thank God for His mercy, which doesn't require that your visible eye see beyond the present moment. Life is to be a moment-by-moment walk with God, not a marathon race. You don't know what the night will bring, but you can trust Him Who made both the day and night. John Alfred

Brashear, lensmaker and astronomer, wrote for his and his wife's gravestone, ''We have loved the stars too fondly to be fearful of the night.'' [7] That's living in the now. This moment is all we've got, and we *can* have faith without fear.

Why is the light of faith so often dim? J. Wallace Hamilton, an imaginative, compassionate preacher now with the Lord, used to answer that query by stating, ''If you want to believe, you have to stand where the light is shining.'' [8] If you want faith, go where other men and women have found it and expose yourself with some measure of regularity to the contagion of other people's faith.

This means that one does not absend himself from fellowshipping with other believers. This means that one goes to the light of the Word. Hamilton calls Thomas, one of the disciples, the spiritual ancestor of the absentee, the man who wasn't there, the patron saint of a whole generation of Thomases living in a fog, wanting more faith. Why? Because they have detached themselves from the Christian fellowship, the community of Christians who can be walking love and the means God often chooses to use to help us in our pilgrimage here on planet Earth.

Thomas was not with Jesus' other disciples that night in the upper room when Jesus presented Himself to them where they had assembled in fear. It was after His crucifixion, after His bodily resurrection.

The disciples were meeting behind locked doors, in fear of the Jewish leaders, when suddenly Jesus was standing there among them! He showed them his hands and side. And how wonderful was their joy as they saw their Lord!

One of the disciples, Thomas, ''The Twin,'' was not there at the time with the others. When they kept telling him, ''We have seen the Lord,'' he replied, ''I won't believe it unless I see the nail wounds in his hands—and put my fingers into them—and place my hand into his side.''

Eight days later the disciples were together again, and this time Thomas was with them. The doors were locked; but suddenly, as before, Jesus was standing among them and greeting them.

Then he said to Thomas, ''Put your finger into my hands. Put your hand into my side. *Don't be faithless any longer. Believe!*'' (John 20:19-27). (Author's italics.)

HOW DOES A PERSON MOVE FROM UNBELIEF TO FAITH?

What was Thomas's response? Immediate belief. Up until that moment Thomas brooded in lonely solitude, burying his despair in hopelessness. His unbelief and lack of faith reached a terrible climax. He was gripped by the obsession that he could not possibly believe these wild tales that Jesus was alive and had appeared to the disciples unless he could see it for himself. He thought he had to see to believe.

More than half the world is Thomas, afraid to believe. Half of every human heart is Thomas . . . A man is at fault in his unbelief when, like Thomas, he stands in his own light; when he won't come where the light is; or when he won't expose his mind to the light. Look at him—this chronic doubter . . . Thomas, one of the twelve, was absent when Jesus came (the first time). The man who missed the moment missed the Lord. Thomas lived for a week in the shadows of dark despondency, because he wasn't in the place where he was most likely to meet the Lord. 9

How does a person move from unbelief to belief? From faithlessness, like Thomas, to faith? From the shadows of suicide to the light?

We cheat ourselves because we react negatively in unbelief to emotional doubts that cloud the horizon. Our insistence on facts regarding this thing called faith and belief, when in many other matters we believe even when we can't see, corrodes our thinking with dark fears. How grateful we should be for our amazing five senses. They tell us much, these little gateways through which the physical world invades our consciousness. Yet there is so much unseen that is real and utterly beyond our sensory perception. Hamilton gives a particularly apt illustration that confirms this. He says:

"The world, scientists say, is made of atoms. What do they mean, atoms? Show us some; let us see an atom. We don't see atoms; we believe in them. We believe in what we can't see. And men who couldn't see an atom, split it. We can't see energy, gravity, electricity—the invisible link between cause and affect. How many things we believe with confidence which we never expect to see at all. We have never seen an idea, felt a truth, or put a finger on a thought. The whole world of the mind, almost everything that is basic in personality—all of it is invisible to our eyes as God is invisible.

So people to whom seeing is believing—who don't believe until they can touch and see—are in a bad way; they live in too small a world; more than that, they live in a deceptive world. Thomas thought that at least he could trust his senses; what he could see and touch, he could believe. But we have learned how deceptive the senses are and how little they can grasp and how much insight it takes to get back of the way things appear to the way they actually are. Our senses fool us, even in small things. To us this desk is solid, but the scientists say it isn't—it is nothing but empty space with electrons whirling around, structured to appear solid. Our eyes tell us that the world is flat, but we know it isn't; that the sun rises, but we know it doesn't, and that the sky is blue, but the color is only optical illusion. Even the beautiful redness of the rose is not real, only a delightful deception of the optic nerve. You can't trust your senses. They don't tell you the whole truth about anything. [10]

Hamilton reminds us that we need to remember that our senses are not adequate; they cannot grasp enough of anything to give us the whole truth about it. He uses the illustration of a ship sailing out to sea and off there, on what we call the horizon, it disappears—it's gone. The horizon isn't real, it's only the limit of our vision, the place beyond which our sight cannot go. If we could only see a little farther, we would know the truth, that the ship is just as big and just as real as when it left the harbor.

Hamilton goes on to explain, *"Well, that is our faith. We believe where we cannot see. We trust in Christ beyond the horizon. We believe His goodness, beyond our sight. We trust His Word against the optic nerve."* [11] (Author's italics.)

That is my answer, too, for the doubting Thomases today, for those inclined to feel like throwing in the towel and calling it quits. Jesus said something that day to Thomas about you and me—yes, about us. Jesus told Thomas, "You believe because you have seen me. But blessed are those who haven't seen me and believe anyway" (John 20:29).

We have not seen Jesus or touched Him. We have not heard Him speak in an audible voice even though we claim He answers our prayers. Have you seen Him, heard Him, or touched Him?

"The things which are seen," said the Apostle Paul, "are temporal; but the things which are not seen are eternal" (2 Corinthians 4:18, *KJV*).

Paul's answer to the person who is filled with doubts and despairing of life is this: "Do not look at what [you] can see right now, the troubles all around [you], but look forward to the joys in heaven which [you] have not yet seen. The troubles will soon be over, but the joys to come will last forever" (2 Corinthians 4:18).

LOST, WANDERING SHEEP NEED A SHEPHERD

Christ came into this world that we might have life and that we might have it more abundantly. He explained this so beautifully in the parable of the Good Shepherd, where He speaks of sheep recognizing the voice and following the Shepherd and of the thief coming into the sheepfold with the purpose of stealing, killing, and destroying. Jesus said:

My purpose is to give life in all its fullness. I am the Good Shepherd. The Good Shepherd lays down his life for the sheep . . . The Father loves me because I lay down my life that I may have it back again. No one can kill me without my consent—I lay down my life voluntarily. For I have the right and power to lay it down when I want to and also the right and power to take it again. For the Father has given me this right (John 10:10b, 11, 17, 18).

We are actually very much like lost wandering sheep. Jesus' illustration, as with all His parables, so perfectly fitted the need to which He was addressing Himself. In lonely desperation, there are those who wander aimlessly, shepherdless. Such as these are easy prey for that thief of thieves, Satan himself, who would snatch them away into death. No wonder David the psalmist said:

The Lord is my shepherd; I shall not want. He maketh me to lie down in green pastures; he leadeth me beside the still waters. He restoreth my soul; he leadeth me in the paths of righteousness for his name's sake. Yea, though I walk through the valley of the shadow of death, I will fear no evil: for thou art with me; thy rod and thy staff they comfort me. Thou preparest a table before me in the presence of mine enemies: thou annointest my head with oil; my cup runneth over. Surely goodness and mercy shall follow me all the days of my life: and I will dwell in the house of the Lord forever (Psalm 23, *KJV*).

Because David knew God as a Shepherd, he was conscious of God's leading, even through valleys—the valley of the shadow of death itself—and with God guarding, guiding, providing, protecting, David knew that whatever happened was God's will. Even though it might appear unbelievably agonizing, terribly traumatic, all wrong and senseless, still God was in it, and David could speak of God's goodness and unfailing kindness. That kind of trusting and believing will take a person through the darkest of valleys.

THE MEANS FOR ESCAPE

I commend this kind of a God to you, the reader. Life is often a long, grim race. But you don't have to run it alone. Jesus is always there, ready to forgive our sins, remove our guilt, and hold on to us when we are tempted to let go.

If you were hanging by your fingernails to the edge of a cliff, close to losing your last hold on your mortal life, and someone came along who could grab your hand and rescue you from almost certain death, you'd let him hold on to you and save your life, wouldn't you? That is the picture of what God through Christ has done. In our sinful, lost state, God reached out, because He cared, because He loved us, and took our hands.

The Bible says that we are all facing an impending danger—the danger of eternal separation from everything that is good and worthwhile. Sin, anything opposite of what God wants, pulls us over the edge of the spiritual cliff. Our grip may be strong enough to hang on for a short time but not strong enough to pull ourselves up to safety. God knows that we are all strung out on the very brink of disaster; in fact, He sent His Son Jesus (even His Name means Savior) to provide us a way to be rescued from a fate that is literally worse than death—eternal separation from Him. God doesn't make us take Jesus' hand, however, but He does provide the means for escape.

WHAT IS THE ANSWER?

If some of you reading this are hanging onto life by your fingernails, as it were, on this brink of disaster, thinking perhaps of suicide as an escape and the way out, and you choose not to accept

God's salvation and grasp onto the Reality of Jesus, then you will be committing eternal suicide. But if you will just place yourself into the Savior's hands, He will never let you go; He will save you. Jesus will tell you where to place your feet. He will endow you with inner resources capable of meeting every need and confronting every situation.

If it is true that the death of love evokes the love of death, then accept the fact that Jesus loves you with a love that far surpasses any earthly love of any human being and that in His love you can live and face the rest of today and the tomorrows. With this new identity in Christ you will gain security. You will "belong" to the family of God, and you will be loved. "I, even I, am He who comforts you . . . What right have you to fear mortal men?" (Isaiah 51:12).

Psychiatrist Viktor Frankl has said, "Until a man has found meaning in death, he cannot hope to find meaning in life." There can be no meaningful death unless we are God's through Christ, and there can be no meaning in life so long as a man is not in Christ.

What then is the answer to living and dying? It is not *people*, but it is the power and help that come from God. It has been proven, as stated earlier in this book, that hope moves a person out of suicidal preoccupation. I recognize, however, that hope must be based on reality factors. Let there be the recognition then that life is not all beauty and joy. God's comfort and love is not a luxurious davenport, breakfast in bed, air-conditioning, a new car, or other external extras that may make living a little more enjoyable but not necessarily provide internal comfort.

God's comfort can make you strong in weakness. He may not take away your problems and He may not remove the Cross, but He will give you strength to bear it. He may not remove you from the battle, but He will give peace in the midst of personal war. He does not always remove adversity, but He gives courage to endure. Darkness and light, joy and sorrow, success and suffering—all of these are indispensable strands in the texture of existence.[12] But in and through it all, here is the ultimate answer: "Hope in God" (Psalm 42:5).

"Why art thou cast down, O my soul?" the psalmist asked. And we ask it too. "Why art thou disquieted in me? Why downcast? Why be discouraged and sad? Why be depressed and gloomy? Trust in God! Praise Him for His wonderous help; He will make you smile again'' (paraphrase of Psalm 42:5; 43:5). Yes, I strongly recommend this: *''Hope in God.''*

1. J. Wallace Hamilton, *What About Tomorrow?* (Old Tappan, N.J.: Fleming H. Revell Co., 1972).

2 .Maurice L. Farber, *Theory of Suicide* (New York: Funk and Wagnalls, 1968).

3. ''Go to the Top for Help,'' *These Times* (November, 1972).

4. Sylvia Plath, *The Bell Jar,* (New York: Harper and Row, 1971).

5. Ibid.

6. Alvarez, *The Savage God.*

7. Kenneth L. Wilson, *Have Faith Without Fear* (New York: Harper and Row, 1970).

8. J. Wallace Hamilton, *What About Tomorrow?* (Old Tappan, N.J.: Felming H. Revell Co., 1972).

9. Ibid., p. 59.

10. Ibid., pp. 63-64.

11. Ibid., p. 65.

12. Earl A. Grollman, *Suicide.*

Appendix

CONTACT
Teleministries U.S.A.

PHONE NUMBERS—CONTACT TELEMINISTRIES U.S.A.

ALABAMA:
So. Baldwin County: Foley   205/943-5675

ARKANSAS:
Hot Springs	501/623-2515
Little Rock	501/666-0234
Malvern	501/337-0500
Pine Bluff	501/536-4226

CALIFORNIA:
Contra Costa County:	Lafayette	415/284-2273
	Walnut Creek	415/923-4357
	Other Places	415/Enterprise 1-6204
Garden Grove		714/639-4673
Lake Arrowhead		714/337-4300
Los Angeles		213/620-0144
Pasadena		213/449-4500
Sacramento		916/452-8255
San Jose		408/266-8228

DELAWARE:
Wilmington   302/575-1112

GEORGIA:
Atlanta   404/261-3644

ILLINOIS:
Rockford	815/964-4044
Polo	815/Enterprise 1566

INDIANA:
Anderson		317/649-5211
Lake County:	Gary/Merrillville	219/769-3141
	Cedar Lake	219/374-7660
New Albany/Jeffersonville		812/945-1167
White County:	Monticello	219/583-4357
	Brookston/Chalmers	219/Enterprise 4357

MARYLAND:
Baltimore   301/332-1114

MINNESOTA:
  Minneapolis/St. Paul   612/341-2896

MISSISSIPPI:
  Columbus   601/328-0200
  Choctaw, Clay, Lowndes, Noxubee, Oktibbeha,
  Webster and Winston Counties: Columbus   601/328-0200
  Jackson   601/969-7272

MISSOURI:
  St. Charles   314/Enterprise 41143
  St. Louis   314/725-3022

NEW JERSEY:
  Atlantic County: Linwood   609/646-6616
  Burlington County: Willingboro   609/871-4700
                     Moorestown   609/234-8888
                     Mt. Holly   609/267-8500
                   . Riverside   609/461-4700
  Camden County: Cherry Hill   609/667-3000
                 Berlin, Pine Hill   609/428-2900
  Cape May County   609/398-6668
  Cumberland County: Bridgeton   609/455-3280
  Gloucester County: Glassboro   609/881-6200
                     Pitman   609/468-6200
  Hudson County: Jersey City   201/332-0236
  Mercer County: Highstown   609/585-2244
                 Princeton   609/896-2120
                 Trenton   609/888-2111
  Monmouth County: Long Branch   201/222-2233
  Ocean County: Toms River   201/349-5367
  Salem County: Salem   609/935-4357
  Scotch Plains   201/232-2880
  Union-Essex Counties: Union   201/527-0555

NEW YORK:
  New York City   212/481-1070
  Syracuse   315/445-1500

NORTH CAROLINA::
Charlotte	704/333-6121
Durham	919/683-1595
Fayetteville	919/485-4134
High Point	919/882-8121
Johnston County: Smithfield	919/934-6161
Lexington	704/249-8974
Randolph County: Asheboro	919/629-0313
Rocky Mount	919/443-5144
Union County: Marshville	704/624-2044
Monroe	704/289-5390
Winston-Salem	919/722-5153

OHIO:
Ashtabula County: Ashtabula	216/998-2607
Conneaut, Geneva	216/Enterprise 2607
Cincinnati	513/631-0111
Crawford County: Bucyrus	419/562-9010
Galion	419/468-9081
Other Places	419/Enterprise 9081
Trumbull County: Girard, Niles	216/545-4371
Warren	216/393-1565
Other Places	216/Enterprise 1565

OKLAHOMA:
Enid	405/234-1111
Grant County	405/234-1111 (COLLECT)
Perry	405/Enterprise 53620
Oklahoma City	405/236-0551

PENNSYLVANIA:
Chambersburg	717/264-7799
Franklin and Fulton Counties	717/Enterprise 7799
Cornwells Heights	215/245-1442
Harrisburg	717/652-4400
Lancaster	717/299-4855
Lancaster County	717/Enterprise 100-39
Chester County	717/Enterprise 100-39
New Castle	412/658-5529
Philadelphia	215/879-4402

Pennsylvania: continued)

Pittsburgh	412/782-4024
York	717/845-3656
York County	717/Enterprise 9830

SOUTH CAROLINA:
Columbia	803/782-9222
Lancaster	803/285-7914

TENNESSEE:
Chattanooga	615/622-5193
Cleveland	615/479-9666
Kingsport	615/246-2273
Hawkins County	615/272-2276
Knoxville	615/523-9124
Marion County	615/658-5005
McMinn/Meigs Counties: Athens	615/745-9111
Oak Ridge	615/482-4949

TEXAS:
Arlington/Fort Worth	817/277-2233
Dallas	214/361-6624
Lubbock	806/765-8393

VIRGINIA:
Franklin and Patrick Counties	703/Enterprise 605
Henry County: Martinsville	703/632-7295
James City County: Williamsburg	804/874-7279
Newport News	804/245-0041
Petersburg	804/733-1100
Virginia Beach	804/428-2211

WEST VIRGINIA:
Beckley	304/252-7817
Charleston	304/346-0826
Huntington	304/523-3448
Oak Hill	304/469-2944

Note: Reprinted by permission of Contact Teleministries, U.S.A., Inc. 900 S. Arlington Avenue, Harrisburg, Pennsylvania 17109.

Suicide Prevention Centers

Directory of Suicide Prevention/Crisis
Agencies in the United States

(Courtesy American Association of Suicidology)

SUICIDE PREVENTION CENTERS

ALABAMA

*CRISIS CENTER OF JEFFERSON COUNTY, INC.
3600-8th Avenue South
Birmingham, Alabama 35222
Director: Edward B. Speaker
Emergency Telephone: (205) 323-7777
Business Telephone: same

NORTH CENTRAL ALABAMA CRISIS CALL CENTER
304-4th Avenue S.E.
Decatur, Alabama 35601
Director: Raymond C. McCaslin
Emergency Telephone: (205) 355-8000
Business Telephone: (205) 355-8505

MUSCLE SHOALS MENTAL HEALTH CENTER
635 West College Street
Florence, Alabama 35630
Director: Thomas Pirkle
Emergency Telephone: (205) 764-3431
Business Telephone: same

ALASKA

*SUICIDE PREVENTION & CRISIS CENTER
825 L Street
Anchorage, Alaska 99501
President: James A. Smith, Jr.
Emergency Telephone: (907) 277-0222
Business Telephone: (907) 277-0027

ARIZONA

MENTAL HEALTH SERVICES SUICIDE PREVENTION CENTER
1825 East Roosevelt
Phoenix, Arizona 85006
Chief: James E. Matters
Emergency Telephone: (602) 258-6301
Business Telephone: (602) 258-6381

*SUICIDE PREVENTION/CRISIS CENTER
801 South Prudence Road
Tucson, Arizona 85710
Director: Jim Tillema
Emergency Telephone: (602) 795-0123
Business Telephone: same

CALIFORNIA

MARILYN ADAMS SUICIDE PREVENTION CENTER OF BAKERSFIELD, INC.
800-11th Street
Bakersfield, California 93304
Executive Secretary: Sylvia Prestige
Emergency Telephone: (805) 325-1232
Business Telephone: none

SUICIDE PREVENTION OF SANTA CRUZ COUNTY, INC.
P.O. Box 36
Ben Lomond, California 95005
Director: Rev. Warren Howell
Emergency Telephone: (408) 426-2342
Business Telephone: (408) 688-1111

SUICIDE PREVENTION OF ALAMEDA COUNTY, INC.
P.O. Box 9102
Berkeley, California 94709
Director: Dr. Ronald Tauber
Emergency Telephone: (415) 849-2212
(415) 537-1323
Business Telephone: (415) 848-1515
(415) 573-1324

*SUICIDE PREVENTION AND CRISIS CENTER OF SAN MATEO COUNTY
1811 Trousdale Drive
Burlingame, California 94010
Director: Charlotte Ross
Emergency Telephone: (415) 877-5600
(415) 367-8000
(415) 726-5581
Business Telephone: (415) 877-5604

*MONTEREY COUNTY SUICIDE PREVENTION CENTER
P.O. Box 3241
Carmel, California 93921
Director: Elizabeth Corr
Emergency Telephone: (408) 649-8008
Business Telephone: (408) 375-6966

HELP LINE, INC.
P.O. Box 5658
China Lake, California 93555
Director: Joe McIntire
Emergency Telephone: (714) 446-5531
Business Telephone: same

*SUICIDE PREVENTION OF DAVIS
618 Sunset Court
Davis, California 95616
Director: Patricia Allen
Emergency Telephone: (916) 756-5000
Business Telephone: same

CRISIS HOUSE
126 W. Main Street
El Cajon, California 92021
Director: James Keeley
Emergency Telephone: (714) 444-1194
Business Telephone: same

SADDLEBACK VALLEY "HELP LINE"
El Toro, California 92630
President: Robert Adams
Emergency Telephone: (714) 830-2522

HELP IN EMOTIONAL TROUBLE
P.O. Box 468
Fresno, California 93721
Director: Caryl Gill
Emergency Telephone: (805) 485-1432
Business Telephone: (805) 264-0386

HOT LINE—GARDEN GROVE
c/o Garden Grove Counseling Service
12345 Euclid Street
Garden Grove, California 92640
Director: Dr. Glen H. McCormick
Emergency Telephone: (714) 636-2424
Business Telephone: (714) 636-1060

NEW HOPE 24-HOUR COUNSELING SERVICE
12141 Lewis Street
Garden Grove, California 92640
Director: Dr. Raymond E. Beckering
Emergency Telephone: (714) 639-4673
Business Telephone: (714) 534-0275

"HELP NOW" LINE
2750 Bellflower Blvd., Suite 204
Long Beach, California 90815
Director: Robert F. Gunter
         Tom Stockton
Emergency Telephone: (213) 435-7669
Business Telephone: (213) 595-2353
                     (213) 595-2354

HELP LINE CONTACT CLINIC
427 West Fifth Street, Suite 500
Los Angeles, California 90013
Directors: Lloyd T. Workman
           Clyde Reynolds
           J. David Gray
Emergency Telephone: (213) 620-0144
Business Telephone: (213) 620-0148

LOS ANGELES FREE CLINIC
115 North Fairfax
Los Angeles, California 90036
Director: Mark Edelstein
Emergency Telephone: (213) 935-9669
Business Telephone: (213) 938-9141

**SUICIDE PREVENTION CENTER
1041 So. Menlo Avenue
Los Angeles, California 90006
Director: Sam M. Heilig
Emergency Telephone: (213) 386-5111
Business Telephone: same

NORTH BAY SUICIDE PREVENTION, INC.
P.O. Box 2444
Napa, California 94558
Director: Susan Thomas
Emergency Telephone: (707) 643-2555
                     (707) 255-2555
                     (707) 963-2555

SUICIDE PREVENTION AND
CRISIS INTERVENTION CENTER
101 South Manchester Avenue
Orange, California 92668
Director: Dr. Carlos Munoz-Mellowes
Emergency Telephone: (714) 633-9393
Business Telephone: same

SUICIDE CRISIS INTERVENTION
CENTER
c/o Palm Springs Mental Health Clinic
1720 East Vista Chino
Palm Springs, California 92262
Coordinator: Georgia Winkler
Emergency Telephone: (714) 346-9502
Business Telephone: (714) 327-8426

PASADENA MENTAL HEALTH
ASSOCIATION
1815 North Fair Oaks
Pasadena, California 91103
Administrator: Dr. Malcolm Coffee
Emergency Telephone: (213) 798-0907
Business Telephone: (213) 681-1381

PSYCHIATRIC CRISIS CLINIC
Sacramento Medical Center Emergency
Area
2315 Stockton Boulevard
Sacramento, California 95817
Chief: Dr. Richard Yarvis
Emergency Telephone: (916) 454-5707
Business Telephone: same

*SUICIDE PREVENTION SERVICE
SACRAMENTO COUNTY, INC.
P.O. Box 449
Sacramento, California 95802
Director: Dr. Richard Brooks
Emergency Telephone: (916) 481-2233
Business Telephone: (916) 481-4433

MARIN SUICIDE PREVENTION
CENTER
P.O. Box 792
San Anselmo, California 94960
Director: Dr. Richard Reubin
Emergency Telephone: (415) 454-4524
Business Telephone: (415) 454-4525

SUICIDE PREVENTION SERVICE
1999 North "D" Street
San Bernardino, California 92405
Director: Phyllis Plate
Emergency Telephone: (714) 886-4880
Business Telephone: (714) 882-4510

*DEFY Counseling Line
2870 4th Avenue
San Diego, California 92103
Director: Maria T. Morales
Emergency Telephone: (714) 236-3339
Business Telephone: same

HELP CENTER
5069 College Avenue
San Diego, California 92115
Emergency Telephone:(714)582-HELP
Business Telephone: (714) 582-4442

SUICIDE PREVENTION, INC.
307-12th Avenue
San Francisco, California 94118
Director: Roger Cornut
Emergency Telephone: (415) 221-1424
Business Telephone: (415) 752-4866

CENTER FOR SPECIAL PROBLEMS
2107 Van Ness Avenue
San Francisco, California 94109
Director: Dr. Eugene Turrell
Emergency Telephone: (415) 558-4801
Business Telephone: same

SUICIDE AND CRISIS SERVICE
645 So. Bascom Avenue
San Jose, California 95128
Coordinator: Lucia Chambers
Emergency Telephone: (408) 287-2424
Business Telephone: (408) 286-5442

NORTH BAY SUICIDE PRE-
VENTION
401 Amador Street
Vallejo, California 94590
President: Susan Thomas
Emergency Telephone: (707) 643-2555
Business Telephone: none

SUICIDE PREVENTION SERVICE
c/o Mental Health Association
33 Chrisman
Ventura, California 93003
Director: Dr. Andrew Morrison
Emergency Telephone: (805) 648-2444
Business Telephone: (805) 648-5071

SUICIDE PREVENTION-CRISIS
  INTERVENTION
P.O. Box 4852
Walnut Creek, California 94596
Director: Philip Lang
Emergency Telephone: (415) 939-3232
Business Telephone: (415) 939-1916

COLORADO

ARAPAHOE   MENTAL   HEALTH
  CENTER
551 Lansing
Aurora, Colorado 80010
Director: Dr. Thomas Nelson
Emergency Telephone: (303) 761-0620

SUICIDE REFERRAL SERVICE
P.O. Box 4438
Colorado Springs, Colorado 80930
Director: Kenneth W. Felts
Emergency Telephone: (303) 471-4357
Business Telephone: none

EMERGENCY PSYCHIATRIC SER-
  VICE
Colorado General Hospital
4200 East Ninth Avenue
Denver, Colorado 80220
Director: Mark W. Rhine
Emergency Telephone: (303) 394-8297
Business Telephone: none

EMERGENCY   ROOM   PSY-
  CHIATRIC SERVICES
Denver General Hospital
West 8th Avenue & Bannock
Denver, Colorado 80206
Director: Glenn Swank
Emergency Telephone: (303) 244-6835
Business Telephone: (303) 893-7001

SUICIDE AND CRISIS CONTROL
2459 South Ash
Denver, Colorado 80222
Director: Rev. Bill Anderson
Emergency Telephone: (303) 746-8485
Business Telephone: same

ARAPAHOE   MENTAL · HEALTH
  CENTER
4857 South Broadway
Englewood, Colorado 80110
Director: Dr. Thomas Nelson
Emergency Telephone: (303) 761-0620
Business Telephone: same

CRISIS   CENTER   AND   SUICIDE
  PREVENTION SERVICE
599-Thirty Road
Grand Junction, Colorado 81501
Director: Don G. Sperber
Emergency Telephone: (303) 242-0577
Business Telephone: same

'SUICIDE PREVENTION CENTER
401 Michigan
Pueblo, Colorado 81001
Director: Layton P. Zimmer
Emergency Telephone: (303) 544-1133
Business Telephone: (303) 544-0904
                                        x. 42

DELAWARE

PSYCHIATRIC EMERGENCY TELE-
  PHONE SERVICE
Sussex   County   Community   Mental
  Health Center
Beebe Hospital of Sussex County
Lewes, Delaware 19958
Director: Dr. Lion DeBernard
Emergency Telephone: (302) 856-6626
Business Telephone: (302) 856-6108

PSYCHIATRIC EMERGENCY SER-
  VICE
2001   North   DuPont   Parkway,
  Farnburst
New Castle, Delaware 19720
Director: Dr. Aydin Z. Bill
Emergency Telephone: (302) 656-4428
Business Telephone: (302) 654-5121

WASHINGTON, D.C.

AMERICAN UNIVERSITY MULTI-
PLE EMERGENCY CENTER
Mary Graydon Center, Room 316
Washington, D.C. 20016
Director: Dr. Alan Berman
         Dr. Barry McCarthy
Emergency Telephone: (202) 966-9511
Business Telephone: (202) 966-9513

SUICIDE   PREVENTION   AND
    EMERGENCY   MENTAL
    HEALTH SERVICE
801 North Capitol Street, N.E.
Washington, D.C. 20002
Director: Phyllis Clemmons
Emergency Telephone: (202) 629-5222
Business Telephone: (202) 347-7041

FLORIDA

**ALACHUA   COUNTY   CRISIS
    CENTER
606 S.W. 3rd Avenue
Gainesville, Florida 32601
Director: Dr. Joe D. Thigpen
Emergency Telephone: (904) 376-4444
Business Telephone: (904) 372-3659

**SUICIDE PREVENTION CENTER
P.O. Box 6393
Jacksonville, Florida 32205
Director: Bonnie Jacob
Emergency Telephone: (904) 384-6488
Business Telephone: (904) 384-3344

PERSONAL CRISIS SERVICE
30 S. E. 8th Street
Miami, Flordia 33131
Director: Nina Poschlevaite
Emergency Telephone: (305) 379-2611
Business Telephone: (305) 379-3642

* WE CARE, INC.
610 Mariposa
Orlando, Florida 32801
Coordinator: Kathy Anderson
Emergency Telephone: (305) 241-3329
Business Telephone: (305) 423-9531

ROCKLEDGE CRISIS AND SUICIDE
    INTERVENTION SERVICE
Brevard County Mental Health Center
1770 Cedar Street
Rockledge, Florida 32955
Director: Harold E. Frank
Emergency Telephone: (305) 784-2433
Business Telephone: (305) 632-9480

CRISIS   INTERVENTION   OF
    SARASOTA
1650 S. Osprey Avenue
Sarasota, Florida 33578
Director: Jane Barry
Emergency Telephone: (813) 959-6686
Business Telephone: none

ADULT MENTAL HEALTH CLINIC
Pinellas County
630-6th Avenue South
St. Petersburg, Florida 33711
Director: Edward Meares
Emergency Telephone: (813) 347-0392
Business Telephone: (813) 347-2108

*SUICIDE AND CRISIS CENTER OF
    TAMPA
1723 W. Kennedy Blvd. #103
Tampa, Florida 33606
Director: Carlos A. Perez
Emergency Telephone: (813) 253-3311
Business Telephone: (813) 251-9200

CRISIS LINE
707 Chillingworth Drive
West Palm Beach, Florida 33401
Director: Robert K. Alsofrom, Ph.D.
Emergency Telephone: (305) 848-8686
Business Telephone: (305) 399-2244

GEORGIA

FULTON COUNTY EMERGENCY
    MENTAL HEALTH SERVICE
99 Butler Street, S.E.
Atlanta, Georgia 30303
Director: Richard Lyles, Ph.D.
Emergency Telephone: (404) 572-2626
Business Telephone: same

DeKALB EMERGENCY AND CRISIS
INTERVENTION SERVICES
Central DeKalb Mental Health Center
500 Winn Way
Decatur, Georgia 30030
Director: Jane Yates, R.N., M.N.
Emergency Telephone: (404) 292-1137
Business Telephone: (404) 202-5231

CARROLL CRISIS INTERVENTION
CENTER
201 Presbyterian Avenue
Carrollton, Georgia 30117
Director: Stephen B. Blanchette
Emergency Telephone: (404) 834-3326
Business Telephone: (404) 834-3327

HELP LINE
1512 Bull Street
Savannah, Georgia 31401
Director: Dr. Daniel Johnston
Emergency Telephone: (912) 232-3383
Business Telephone: (912) 233-0146

HAWAII

*SUICIDE AND CRISIS CENTER OF
VOLUNTEER INFORMATION
AND REFERRAL SERVICE
200 North Vineyard Boulevard
Room 603
Honolulu, Hawaii 96817
Director: Jean A. Lee
Emergency Telephone: (808) 521-4555
Business Telephone: (808) 536-7234

ILLINOIS

*CALL FOR HELP-INTERVENTION
CENTER
7812 West Main
Belleville, Illinois 62223
Director: Sr. Jo An Pisel
Emergency Telephone: (618) 397-0963
Business Telephone: (618) 397-0968

CHAMPAIGN COUNTY SUICIDE
PREVENTION & CRISIS SERVICE
1206 South Randolph
Champaign, Illinois 61820
Director: Betty Lazarus
Emergency Telephone: (217) 359-4141
Business Telephone: (217) 352-7921

CRISIS INTERVENTION PROGRAM
4200 North Oak Park Avenue
Chicago, Illinois 60634
Director: Helen Sunukjian, Ph.D.
Emergency Telephone: (312) 794-3609
Business Telephone: (312) 794-4230

CRISIS COUNSELING SERVICE
Jefferson County Mental Health Center
1300 Salem Road
Mt. Vernon, Illinois 62864
Director: James L. Nicholson, M.S.
Emergency Telephone: (618) 242-1511
Business Telephone: (618) 242-1510

CALL FOR HELP
320 E. Armstrong Avenue
Peoria, Illinois 61603
Director: Mrs. Barbara Runyan
Emergency Telephone: (309) 691-7373
Business Telephone: (309) 673-6481
                                            ext. 21

SUICIDE PREVENTION SERVICE
520 South 4th Street
Quincey, Illinois 62301
Director: Robert Scott, ACSW
Emergency Telephone: (217) 222-1166
Business Telephone: (217) 223-0413

OPEN LINE SERVICE
114 East Cherry Street
Watseka, Illinois 60970
Director: Anthony Flore, M.S.
Emergency Telephone: (815) 432-5111
Business Telephone: (815) 432-5241

INDIANA

SUICIDE PREVENTION SERVICE—
   MARION COUNTY ASSOC. FOR
   MENTAL HEALTH
1433 North Meridian Street
Indianapolis, Indiana 46202
Director: Patricia C. Jones
Emergency Telephone: (317) 632-7575
Business Telephone: (317) 636-2491

• SUICIDE PREVENTION OF ST.
   JOSEPH COUNTY
532 South Michigan Street
South Bend, Indiana 46601
Director: Tobe Schmucker
Emergency Telephone: (219) 233-1221
Business Telephone: (219) 288-4842

IOWA

LEE COUNTY MENTAL HEALTH
   CENTER
110 North 8th Street
Keokuk, Iowa 52632
Director: Harry D. Harper, M.D.
Emergency Telephone: (319) 524-3873
Business Telephone: same

KANSAS

AREA MENTAL HEALTH CENTER
156 Gardendale
Garden City, Kansas 67846
Director: Harry C. Lester, ACSW
Emergency Telephone: (316) 276-7689
Business Telephone: same

SUICIDE PREVENTION CENTER
250 N. 17
Kansas City, Kansas 66102
Director: Dr. Natalie Hill
Emergency Telephone: (913) 371-7171
Business Telephone: (913) 371-5707

CAN HELP
P.O. Box 4253
Topeka, Kansas 66604
Director: Mrs. Joy Willians
Emergency Telephone: (913) 235-3434
Business Telephone: (913) 232-0437

SUICIDE PREVENTION SERVICE
1045 N. Minneapolis
Wichita, Kansas 67214
Director: Clinton Willsie
Emergency Telephone: (316) 268-8251
Business Telephone: same

LOUISIANA

**BATON ROUGE CRISIS INTER-
   VENTION CENTER
Student Health Service, LSU
Baton Rouge, Louisiana 70803
Director: Myron C. Mohr, Ph.D.
Emergency Telephone:.(504) 388-8222
Business Telephone: (504) 344-0319

*CRISIS LINE
1528 Jackson Avenue
New Orleans, Louisiana 70130
Director: Rick Wagner
Emergency Telephone: (504) 523-2673
Business Telephone: (504) 523-3845

MAINE

DIAL HELP
The Counseling Center
43 Illinois Avenue
Bangor, Maine 04401
Director: Larry Friesen, Ph.D.
Emergency Telephone: (207) 947-0366
Business Telephone: same

BATH-BRUNSWICK AREA RES-
   CUE, INC.
159 Maine Street
Brunswick, Maine 04011
Director: H.B. Carney
Emergency Telephone: (207) 443-3300
Business Telephone: (207) 725-8014

RESCUE, INCORPORATED
331 Cumberland Avenue
Portland, Maine 04101
Director: Rev. Arthur Moore
Emergency Telephone: (207) 774-2767
Business Telephone: (207) 774-4761

MARYLAND

CRISIS INTERVENTION AND PROBLEM SOLVING CLINIC OF SINAI HOSPITAL OF BALTIMORE, INC.
Belvedere Avenue at Greenspring
Baltimore, Maryland 21215
Director: Heull E. Connor, Jr., M.D.
Emergency Telephone: (301) 367-7800
Business Telephone: same ext. 8855
ext. 8846

MONTGOMERY COUNTY HOTLINE
10920 Connecticut Avenue
Kensington, Maryland 20795

MASSACHUSETTS

RESCUE, INC.
115 Southampton Street
Boston, Massachusetts 02118
Director: Rev. Kenneth B. Murphy
Emergency Telephone: (617) 426-6600
Business Telephone: (617) 442-8000

• SAMARITANS OF BOSTON
355 Boylston
Boston, Massachusetts 02138
Director: Monica Dickens
Emergency Telephone: (617) 247-0220
Business Telephone: (617) 536-2460

MICHIGAN

CALL SOMEONE CONCERNED
760 Riverside
Adrian, Michigan
Director: Patricia E. Wentz, M.D.
Emergency Telephone: (313) 263-6737
Business Telephone: (313) 263-2930

COMMUNITY SERVICE CENTER— CHELSEA
775 S. Main Street
Chelsea, Michigan 48118
Director: Mrs. Lucy Howard
Emergency Telephone: (313) 475-2676
Business Telephone: same

**SUICIDE PREVENTION CENTER
1151 Taylor Avenue
Detroit, Michigan 48202
Director: Bruce L. Danto, M.D.
Emergency Telephone: (313) 875-5466
Business Telephone: (313) 872-1830

SUICIDE PREVENTION CRISIS INTERVENTION SERVICE
Community Mental Health Clinic
Ottawa County Building
Room #114
Grand Haven, Michigan 49417
Director: James McDowall, ACSW
Emergency Telephone: (616) 842-4357
Business Telephone: (616) 842-5350

SUICIDE PREVENTION AND CRISIS INTERVENTION SERVICE
5 E. 8th Street
Office 601
Holland, Michigan 49423
Director: Catherine A. Pfeiffer
Emergency Telephone: (616) 396-4537
Business Telephone: (616) 392-1873

DOWNRIVER GUIDANCE CLINIC
Community Crisis Center
1619 Fort Street
Lincoln Park, Michigan 48146
Director: Jean Haslett, M.S.W.
Emergency Telephone: (313)383-9000
Business Telephone: (313) 388-4630
ext. 250

CRISIS CENTER
29200 Hoover Road
Warren, Michigan 48093
Director: Christopher Murphy
Emergency Telephone: (313) 758-6860
Business Telephone: same

YPSILANTI AREA COMMUNITY SERVICES
1637 Holmes Road
Ypsilanti, Michigan 48197
Director: Sr. Sheila Hedegard
Emergency Telephone: (616) 485-0440
Business Telephone: same

MINNESOTA

• CONTACT TWIN CITIES
83 S. 12th Street
Minneapolis, Minnesota
Director: Elaine H. Reid
Emergency Telephone: (612) 341-2212
Business Telephone: same

CRISIS INTERVENTION CENTER
Hennepin County General Hospital
Minneapolis, Minnesota 55415
Director: Zigfrids T. Stelmachers
Emergency Telephone: (612) 330-7777
                                  330-7780
Business Telephone: (612) 330-7950

EMERGENCY SOCIAL SERVICE
413 Auditorium Street
St. Paul, Minnesota 55102
Director: Mrs. Elizabeth K. Undis
Emergency Telephone: (612) 225-1515
Business Telephone: (612) 451-2718
                                  224-4981

CRISIS, INC.
744-19th Avenue, South
South St. Paul, Minnesota 55075
Director: Patrick L. Williams

MISSISSIPPI

LISTENING POST
P.O. Box 2072
Meridian, Mississippi 39301
Director: C. Richard Bahr
Emergency Telephone: (601) 693-1001
Business Telephone: same

MISSOURI

ST. FRANCIS COMMUNITY MEN-
TAL HEALTH CENTER
825 Goodhope
Cape Giardeau, Missouri 63701
Director: Mr. Dale Rauh
Emergency Telephone: (314) 334-6400

WESTERN MISSOURI MENTAL
HEALTH CENTER
Suicide Prevention Center
600 East 22nd Street
Kansas City, Missouri 64108
Director: Nicola Katf, M.D.
Emergency Telephone: None
Business Telephone: (816) 471-3000

CRISIS INTERVENTION, INC.
P.O. Box 582
Joplin, Missouri 64801
Director: Mrs. Jack Carter
Emergency Telephone: (417) 781-2255

ST. JOSEPH SUICIDE PREVENTION
SERVICE
St. Joseph State Hospital
St. Joseph, Missouri 64501
Director: Dward A. Moore
Emergency Telephone: (816) 232-1655
Business Telephone: (816) 232-8431

• LIFE CRISIS SERVICES, INC.
7438 Forsyth
Suite 210
St. Louis, Missouri 63105
Director: Mrs. Gwyn Harvey
Emergency Telephone: (314) 868-6300
Business Telephone: (314) 721-4310

MONTANA

BLACKFEET CRISIS CENTER
Blackfeet Reservation
Browning, Montana 59417
Director: Audra M. Pambrun
Emergency Telephone: (406) 338-5525
                                  226-4291
Business Telephone: (406) 338-5525

GREAT FALLS CRISIS CENTER
P.O. Box 124
Great Falls, Montana 59401
Director: Mr. John Breedon
Emergency Telephone: (406) 453-6511

NEBRASKA

OMAHA PERSONAL CRISIS SERVICE
P.O. Box 1491
Omaha, Nebraska 68101
Director: Billy G. Hartzell
Emergency Telephone: (402) 342-6290
Business Telephone: (402) 292-0839

NEVADA

SUICIDE PREVENTION AND CRISIS CALL CENTER
Room 206 Mack SS Building
University of Nevada
Reno, Nevada 89507
Director: James Mikawa
Emergency Telephone: (702) 323-6111
Business Telephone: (702) 322-8621

NEW HAMPSHIRE

*CENTRAL NEW HAMPSHIRE COMMUNITY HEALTH SERVICES, INC.
#5 Market Lane
Concord, New Hampshire 03301
Director: James O. Wells, Ph.D.
Emergency Telephone: (606) 228-1551
Business Telephone: same

NORTH COUNTY COMMUNITY SERVICES, INC.
227 Main Street
Berlin, New Hampshire 03570
Director: Jack Melton
Emergency Telephone: (603) 752-7404
Emergency Telephone: (603) 752-7404
Business Telephone: (603) 752-4431

NEW JERSEY

ANCORA SUICIDE PREVENTION SERVICE
Ancora Psychiatric Hospital
Hammonton, New Jersey 08037
Director: Leo L. Sell, M.D.
Emergency Telephone: (201) 561-1234
Business Telephone: (201) 561-1700

MIDDLESEX COUNTY-CRISIS INTERVENTION
37 Oakwood Avenue
Metuchen, New Jersey 08840
Director: Doulat Keswani, M.D.
Emergency Telephone: (201) 549-6000
Business Telephone: (201) 549-5711

*SCREENING-CRISIS INTERVENTION PROGRAM
1129B Woodlane Road
Mt. Holly, New Jersey 08060
Director: H. Dillon Crager
Emergency Telephone: (609) 764-1100
Business Telephone: (609) 267-1377

CRISIS, REFERRAL AND INFORMATION
232 E. Front Street
Plainfield, New Jersey 07060
Director: Donald Fell
Emergency Telephone: (201) 561-4800
Business Telephone: (201) 756-3836

NEW MEXICO

*SUICIDE PREVENTION AND CRISIS CENTER OF ALBUQUERQUE, INC.
P.O. Box 4511
Albuquerque, New Mexico 87106
Director: Dorothy Trainor
Emergency Telephone: (505) 265-7557
Business Telephone: (505) 843-2941

THE CRISIS CENTER
Box 3563
University Park Drive
Las Cruces, New Mexico 88001
Director: Byron King
Emergency Telephone: (505) 524-9241
Business Telephone: (505) 524-4081

THE BRIDGE CRISIS INTERVENTION CENTER
113 Bridge Street
Las Vegas, New Mexico 87701
Director: Fran Clark
Emergency Telephone: (505) 425-6793
Business Telephone: (505) 425-5872

NEW YORK

SUICIDE PREVENTION CENTER
Kings County Hospital Center
606 Winthrop Street
Brooklyn, New York 11203
Director: Dr. Eugene Becker
Emergency Telephone: (212) 462-3322
Business Telephone: same

SUICIDE PREVENTION & CRISIS SERVICE, INC.
560 Main Street
Buffalo, New York 14202
Director: Dr. Gene Brockopp
Emergency Telephone: (716) 854-1966
Business Telephone: same

LIFELINE
Nassau County Medical Center
2201 Hempstead Turnpike
East Meadow, New York 11554
Director: Michael King
Emergency Telephone: (516) 538-3111
Business Telephone: (516) 542-3446

*SUICIDE PREVENTION AND CRISIS SERVICE, INC.
P.O. Box 312
Ithaca, New York 14850
Director: Nina Miller
Emergency Telephone: (607) 272-1616
Business Telephone: (607) 272-1505

THE NORMAN VINCENT PEALE TELEPHONE CENTER
3 West 29th Street, 10th Floor
New York, New York 10001
Director: Rev. H. Leslie Christie
Emergency Telephone: (212) 686-3061
Business Telephone: (212) 686-3519

*NATIONAL   SAVE-A-LIFE LEAGUE, INC.
815-2nd Avenue, Suite 409
New York, New York 10017
Director: Harry M. Warren, Jr.
Emergency Telephone: (212) 736-6191
Business Telephone: same

NIAGARA COUNTY CRISIS CENTER
527 Buffalo Avenue
Niagara Falls, New York 14302
Director: Rev. Daniel Clark
Emergency Telephone: (716) 285-3515
Business Telephone: (716) 285-9636

24-HOUR MENTAL HEALTH INFORMATION AND CRISIS PHONE SERVICE
260 Crittenden Boulevard
Rochester, New York 14620
Director: Dr. Haroutun Babigian
Emergency Telephone: (716) 275-4445
Business Telephone: (716) 275-4853

SUICIDE PREVENTION SERVICE
29 Sterling Avenue
White Plains, New York 10606
Director: Elaine S. Feiden
Emergency Telephone: (914) 949-0121
Business Telephone: (914) 949-6741

NORTH CAROLINA

*SUICIDE AND CRISIS SERVICE OF ALAMANCE COUNTY, INC.
P.O. Box 2573
Burlington, North Carolina 27215
Director: Mary Lee Jones
Emergency Telephone: (919) 227-6220
Business Telephone: (919) 228-1720

CRISIS AND SUICIDE CENTER
300 East Main Street
Durham, North Carolina 27701
Director: Mrs. Cobb W. Fox
Emergency Telephone: (919) 688-5504
Business Telephone: (919) 688-4363

CRISIS HELP AND SUICIDE PREVENTION SERVICE OF GASTON COUNTY
508 W. Main Avenue
Gastonia, North Carolina 28052
Director: Yvonne Spencer
Emergency Telephone: (704) 867-6373
Business Telephone: (704) 867-8971

CRISIS CONTROL CENTER, INC.
P.O. Box 735
Greensboro, North Carolina 27402
Director: Gay Tate
Emergency Telephone: (919) 275-2852
Business Telephone: (919) 275-2853

CARE
215 Mill Avenue
Jacksonville, North Carolina 28542
Directors: Artis G. Wood
            Paul Bradford
Emergency Telephone: (919) 346-6292
Business Telephone: (919) 347-5118

SUICIDE AND CRISIS INTERVEN-
TION SERVICE
Halifax County Mental Health
P.O. Box 577
Roanoake Rapids, North Carolina
27870
Director: Soong H. Lee
Emergency Telephone: (919) 537-2909
Business Telephone: (919) 537-6174

CRISIS AND SUICIDE INTER-
VENTION
P.O. Box Q
Sanford, North Carolina 27330
Director: James Hampton
Emergency Telephone: (919) 776-5431
Business Telephone: (919) 775-4129

NORTH DAKOTA

SUICIDE PREVENTION AND
EMERGENCY SERVICE
9th and Thayer
Bismarck, North Dakota 58501
Director: Dr. James O'Toole
Emergency Telephone: (701) 255-4124
Business Telephone: same

SUICIDE PREVENTION AND MEN-
TAL HEALTH CENTER
700 First Avenue, South
Fargo, North Dakota 58102
Director: Dr. Eric Noble
Emergency Telephone: (701) 232-4357
Business Telephone: (701) 237-4513

NORTHEAST REGION MENTAL
HEALTH AND RETARDATION
CENTER
509 South Third Street
Grand Forks, North Dakota 58201
Director: Dr. James Hoyme
Emergency Telephone: (701) 772-7258
Business Telephone: same

ST. JOSEPH'S HOSPITAL SUICIDE
PREVENTION CENTER
St. Joseph's Hospital
Minot, North Dakota 58701
Supervisor: Sister Noemi
Emergency Telephone: (701) 838-5555
Business Telephone: same

OHIO

*SUPPORT, INC.
1361 W. Market Street
Akron, Ohio
Director: Norma Rios
Emergency Telephone: (216) 434-9144
Business Telephone: (216) 864-7743

SUICIDE CONTROL CENTER
Ashtabula General Hospital
505 W. 46th Street
Ashtabula, Ohio 44004
Director: Dr. F. Fournier
Emergency Telephone: (216) 993-6111
Business Telephone: (216) 998-4210

CRISIS INTERVENTION/SUICIDE
PREVENTION
Athens Mental Health Center
Athens, Ohio 45701
Director: Dr. David Caul
Emergency Telephone: (614) 592-3917

SUICIDE PREVENTION AND CRI-
SIS HELP SERVICE
2600 Sixth Street, S.W.
Canton, Ohio 44711
Director: Dr. Herbert Heine
Emergency Telephone: (216) 452-9811
Business Telephone: (216) 452-6000

SUICIDE PREVENTION
1515 E. Broad Street
Columbus, Ohio 43215
Director: Ted Wilson
Emergency Telephone: (614) 221-5445
Business Telephone: (614) 252-0354

SUICIDE PREVENTION SERVICE
1435 Cornell Drive
Dayton, Ohio 45406
Director: Rev. Paul Mills
Emergency Telephone: (513) 223-4777
Business Telephone: (513) 224-1678

TOWN HALL II—HELPLINE
225 E. College Street
Kent, Ohio 44240
Director: Richard Fennig
Emergency Telephone: (216) 672-4357
Business Telephone: (216) 673-4560

RESCUE, INC.
One Stranahan Square
Toledo, Ohio 43624
Director: Mrs. William Hook
Emergency Telephone: (419) 243-4251

CRISIS HOTLINE
2845 Bell Street
Zanesville, Ohio 43701
Director: Dr. Robert Birch
Emergency Telephone: (614) 452-8403
Business Telephone: (614) 452-9121

OREGON

CRISIS SERVICE
127 N. A. Sixth Street
Corvallis, Oregon 97330
Chairman: Mrs. Luke Krygier
Emergency Telephone: (503) 752-7030
Business Telephone: (503) 752-5107

CRISIS CENTER
University of Oregon
Eugene, Oregon 97403
Director: Howard van Arsdale
Emergency Telephone: (503) 686-4488
Business Telephone: same

PENNSYLVANIA

LIFELINE
520 E. Broad Street
Bethlehem, Pennsylvania 18018
Chairman: Dr. A.A. Welsh
Emergency Telephone: (215) 691-0660
Business Telephone: (215) 867-8671

SUICIDE PREVENTION CENTER
Room 430, City Hall Annex
Philadelphia, Pennsylvania 19107
Director: Rose Marie Phillips
Emergency Telephone: (215) 686-4420
Business Telephone: (215) 686-4426

SOUTH CAROLINA

CRISIS INTERVENTION SERVICE
Greenville Area Mental Health
715 Grove Road
Greenville, South Carolina 29605
Director: Rowland Hyde
Emergency Telephone: (803) 239-1021
Business Telephone: (803) 239-1011

TENNESSEE

CRISIS INTERVENTION SERVICE
Helen Ross McNabb Center
1520 Cherokee Trail
Knoxville, Tennessee 37920
Director: Dr. Ken Carpenter
Emergency Telephone: (615) 637-9711

*SUICIDE PREVENTION SERVICE
P.O. Box 4068
Memphis, Tennessee 38104
Director: Mary Puckett
Emergency Telephone: (901) 274-7473
Business Telephone: (901) 324-6669

*CRISIS INTERVENTION CENTER
2311 Elliston Place
Nashville, Tennessee 37203
Director: Ms. Pat Higginbotham
Emergency Telephone: (615) 244-7444
Business Telephone: (615) 327-4235

TEXAS

CALL FOR HELP
P.O. Box 60
Abilene, Texas 79604
Director: Nancy Hutchinson
Emergency Telephone: (915) 673-8211

SUICIDE PREVENTION/CRISIS
  SERVICE
Box 3044
Amarillo, Texas 79106
Director: Mrs. B.H. Rigler
Emergency Telephone: (806) 376-4251
Business Telephone: (806) 376-4431

CONTACT-TARRANT COUNTY
Box 6212
Arlington, Texas 76011
Director: Mary T. Murray
Emergency Telephone: (817) 277-2233
Business Telephone: unlisted

INFORMATION & CRISIS CENTER
2434 Guadalupe
Austin, Texas 78075
Director: Ed Peters
Emergency Telephone: (512) 472-2411
Business Telephone: (512) 478-5695

TELEPHONE COUNSELING AND
  REFERRAL SERVICE
c/o Counseling Center
The University of Texas
P.O. Box 8119
Austin, Texas 78712
Director: Dr. Ira Iscoe
Emergency Telephone: (512) 476-7073
Business Telephone: (512) 471-3515

SUICIDE RESCUE, INC.
5530 Bellaire Lane
Beaumont, Texas 77706
Director: James B. Hutto
Emergency Telephone: (713) 833-2311
Business Telephone: same

SUICIDE PREVENTION/CRISIS
  INTERVENTION
418 West Coolidge
Borger, Texas 79007
Director: Velma Boyd
Emergency Telephone: (806) 274-5389
Business Telephone: (806) 274-5331

CRISIS INTERVENTION SERVICE
P.O. Box 3075
Corpus Christi, Texas 78404
Director: Angela D. Sachson
Emergency Telephone: (512) 883-6244
Business Telephone: (512) 883-0271

SUICIDE PREVENTION OF DAL-
  LAS, INC.
P.O. Box 19651
Dallas, Texas 75219
Director: Charles Vorkoper
Emergency Telephone: (214) 521-5531
Business Telephone: unlisted

DENTON AREA CRISIS CENTER
Flow Memorial Hospital
Room 243, 1310 Scripture Drive
Denton, Texas 76201
Director: Dr. Norma Gilbert
Emergency Telephone: (817)387-HELP
Business Telephone: (817) 382-1612

HELP LINE
P.O. Drawer 1108
Edinburgh, Texas 78539
Director: Bryan Robertson
Emergency Telephone: (512) 383-5341
Business Telephone: (512)383-0121

CRISIS INTERVENTION
730 East Yandell
El Paso, Texas 79902
Director: Gill Lucker
Emergency Telephone: (915) 779-1800
Business Telephone: (915) 532-1481

CRISIS INTERVENTION HOTLINE
212 Burnett
Fort Worth, Texas 76102
Director: John Choate
Emergency Telephone: (817) 336-3355
Business Telephone: (817) 336-5921

CRISIS HOTLINE
P.O. Box 4123
Houston, Texas 77014
Director: Hank Renteria
Emergency Telephone: (713) 228-1505
Business Telephone: (713) 527-9864

CONTACT LUBBOCK, INC.
P.O. Box 3334
Lubbock, Texas 79410
Director: Betty Ross
Emergency Telephone: (806) 765-8393
Business Telephone: (806) 765-7272

SUICIDE RESCUE, INC.
812 West Orange
Orange, Texas 77630
Director: Phyllis Smith
Emergency Telephone: (713) 883-5521
Business Telephone: same

CRISIS CENTER
709 Cliffside
Richardson, Texas 75080
Director: Nancy Novak
Emergency Telephone: (214) 783-0008
Business Telephone: same

CRISIS CENTER
P.O. Box 28061
San Antonio, Texas 78228
Director: Dr. Lawrence Schoenfeld
Emergency Telephone: (512) 732-2141
Business Telephone: (512) 732-9172

CRISIS HELPLINE
Box 57545
Webster, Texas 77598
Director: Katrina Packard
Emergency Telephone: (713) 488-7222
Business Telephone: (713) 488-3528

CONCERN
P.O. Box 1945
Wichita Falls, Texas 76301
Director: Lucille Myers
Emergency Telephone: (817) 723-8231
Business Telephone: same

UTAH

CRISIS INTERVENTION SERVICE
156 Westminister Avenue
Salt Lake City, Utah 84115
Director: Dr. Norman Anderson
Emergency Telephone: (801) 484-8761
Business Telephone: same

VIRGINIA

NORTHERN VIRGINIA HOTLINE
P.O. Box 187
Arlington, Virginia 22210

*SUICIDE-CRISIS CENTER, INC.
3636 High Street
Portsmouth, Virginia 23707
Director: Nancy Mills
Emergency Telephone: (804) 399-6393
Business Telephone: (804) 399-6395

WASHINGTON

CRISIS CLINIC
3423 Sixth Street
Bremerton, Washington 98310
Director: Roger Gray
Emergency Telephone: (206) 373-2402
Business Telephone: (206) 373-7724

EMOTIONAL CRISIS SERVICE
1801 East Fourth
Olympia, Washington 98501
Director: Maxine Knutzen
Emergency Telephone: (206) 357-3681
Business Telephone: (206) 943-4760

*CRISIS CLINIC
1530 Eastlake East
Seattle, Washington 98102
Director: William E. Hershey
Emergency Telephone: (206) 325-5550
Business Telephone: (206) 329-1882

CRISIS SERVICE
107 Division Street
Spokane, Washington 99202
Director: Dr. Z. Nelson
Emergency Telephone: (509) 838-4428
Business Telephone: (509) 838-4651

WEST VIRGINIA

SUICIDE PREVENTION SERVICE
418 Morrison Building
815 Quarrier Street
Charleston, West Virginia 25301
Director: Ted Johnson
Emergency Telephone: (304) 346-3332
Business Telephone: (304) 346-0424

CONTACT HUNTINGTON
520-11th Street
Huntington, West Virginia 25705
Director: Rev. William Miller
Emergency Telephone: (304) 523-3448
Business Telephone: (304) 523-3440

*SUICIDE PREVENTION CENTER
310 Chestnut Street
Eau Claire, Wisconsin 54701
Director: Stuart Thomas
Emergency Telephone: (715) 834-5522
Business Telephone: (715) 839-3217

WALWORTH COUNTY MENTAL
   HEALTH CLINIC
P.O. Box 290
Elkhorn, Wisconsin 53121
Director: Richard Jones
Emergency Telephone: (414) 245-5011
Business Telephone: (414) 723-5400

*EMERGENCY SERVICES DANE
   COUNTY MENTAL HEALTH
   CENTER
31 South Henry Street
Madison, Wisconsin 53703
Director: Bernard Cesnik
Emergency Telephone: (608) 251-2345
Business Telephone: (608) 251-2341

PSYCHIATRIC EMERGENCY SER-
   VICES
8700 W. Wisconsin Avenue
Milwaukee, Wisconsin 53226
Director: Dr. George Currier
Emergency Telephone: (414) 258-2040
Business Telephone: same

WYOMING

HELP LINE, INC.
Cheyenne, Wyoming 82001
Director: Carla Romano
Emergency Telephone: (307) 634-4469

---

*Center members of the American Association of Suicidology as of 11/77.
**Center members certified by the AAS as approved suicide prevention and crisis
   intervention programs as of 11/77.

These centers were obtained from the AAS *Directory of Suicide Prevention/Crisis
Intervention Agencies in the United States*, compiled in 1971.

Notes

Notes